400 blender cocktails

Sensational alcoholic and non-alcoholic cocktail recipes

Andrew Chase, Alison Kent and Nicole Young

Robert
ROSE

For complete cataloging information, see page 256.

Disclaimer
The recipes in this book have been carefully tested by our kitchen and our tasters. To the best of
our knowledge, they are safe and nutritious for ordinary use and users. For those people with food
or other allergies, or who have special food requirements or health issues, please read the suggested
contents of each recipe carefully and determine whether or not they may create a problem for you.
All recipes are used at the risk of the consumer.

We cannot be responsible for any hazards, loss or damage that may occur as a result of any
recipe use.

For those with special needs, allergies, requirements or health problems, in the event of any
doubt, please contact your medical adviser prior to the use of any recipe.

Design & Production: PageWave Graphics Inc.
Editor: Sue Sumeraj
Recipe Tester: Jennifer MacKenzie
Proofreader: Sheila Wawanash
Indexer: Gillian Watts
Photography: Colin Erricson
Food Styling: Kate Bush
Prop Styling: Charlene Erricson

Cover image: Blender Bellini (page 185)

The publisher and author wish to express their appreciation to the following suppliers of props used
in the food photography:

GLASSWARE AND ACCESSORIES

Caban
396 St. Clair Avenue West,
Toronto, Ontario M5P 3N3
Tel: (416) 654-3316
www.caban.ca

Homefront
371 Eglinton Avenue West,
Toronto, Ontario M5N 1A3
Tel: (416) 488-3189
www.homefrontshop.com

We acknowledge the financial support of the Government of Canada through the Book Publishing
Industry Development Program (BPIDP) for our publishing activities.

Published by Robert Rose Inc.
120 Eglinton Avenue East, Suite 800, Toronto, Ontario, Canada M4P 1E2
Tel: (416) 322-6552 Fax: (416) 322-6936

Printed in Canada
1 2 3 4 5 6 7 8 9 CPL 14 13 12 11 10 09 08 07 06

CONTENTS

INTRODUCTION

Blenders are a wonderful tool at the cocktail bar. They chop ice with ease and blend it into frosty concoctions. They allow you to infuse your drinks with fresh or frozen fruit and use frozen juice concentrates to great effect. Rich, sweet cocktails made with ice cream or sorbet widen and simplify your dessert repertoire. You can spike vegetable or fruit smoothies and pretend you're being health-conscious. The blender opens up the world of cocktail innovation like nothing else.

Invite friends over for a blender cocktail party. Stock your bar and buy some seasonal fruits and various ice creams, sorbets and fruit concentrates, then try some of the drinks from this book. Expand your repertoire with original drinks developed in blender cocktail contests with fellow enthusiasts. Most important, enjoy yourself. Blending cocktails isn't a science and shouldn't be made into an art — it's just plain fun.

BLENDER COCKTAIL TIPS

Cleaning Your Blender

To clean your blender, fill it with hot water and let it run for about 1 minute. Then put it in the dishwasher or wash by hand. If your blender base unscrews from the jug, disassemble it, wash the components separately and allow them to dry thoroughly before reassembling. Always rinse your blender between cocktails.

Alcohol Measures

Alcohol is traditionally measured in ounces. Shot glasses are 2-ounce measures, and are often marked with 1- and 1½-ounce measures. One ounce equals 2 tbsp (25 mL); 2 ounces equals ¼ cup (50 mL). In this book, we use ounce measures for alcoholic beverages and regular cooking measures for non-alcoholic ingredients.

Twists

Cocktails are often garnished with citrus twists, strips of twisted citrus rind. To make a citrus twist, cut a strip of rind from the citrus fruit with a sharp paring knife or a peeler, carefully slicing off the peel without the bitter white pith. Twist the strip over the cocktail to release the pungent, fragrant oils in the peel into your drink, or twist and rub the oils over the rim of the glass.

Maraschino Cherries

Maraschino cherries are an essential garnish for the cocktail bar. If they seem a tad unnatural, it is perhaps because they are: to make them, real cherries are stoned and bleached of colour (and most of their taste), then soaked in syrup and bitter almond oil, along with red or green food coloring. It's the almond flavor and the burst of bright color that make them indispensable. For something a bit more natural, during cherry season you can replace maraschino cherries with fresh cherries, each pricked in a few spots with a needle and marinated in almond liqueur (and a splash of kirsch, if you want to be fancy) for 1 to 3 days. Use the leftover marinating liquid as flavoring for your own cocktail inventions.

COCKTAIL SYRUPS

The following syrups are used in recipes throughout the book. Make up a batch of each before your next blender cocktail party so you'll have plenty on hand to use as needed.

Simple Syrup

1 part	granulated sugar
1 part	water

1. In a small saucepan, bring sugar and water to a boil. Boil until sugar is dissolved. Let cool.
2. Pour into a sealable jar or an airtight container. Seal and store at room temperature for up to 1 week.

Honey Syrup

2 parts	honey
1 part	boiling water

1. In a heatproof bowl, stir honey and water until honey is dissolved. Let cool.
2. Pour into a sealable jar or an airtight container. Seal and store in the refrigerator for up to 3 months.

brandy
and cognac

BRANDY DRIVES ITS NAME from the Dutch *brandewijn*, or "burnt wine," although nothing is burnt in its making. However, many drinkers introduced to cheap versions of this spirit experience a decidedly burning sensation when downing it straight. Brandy is distilled wine, but not all brandies are made from grapes. The deservedly famous Calvados, from France, is made from apple cider. Other fruit brandies, such as cherry or apricot brandy, are flavored with fruit extracts and are usually sweetened.

Distilled twice and aged in oak casks, cognac, along with its cousin Armagnac, is the finest brandy. Cognac is produced in the designated Cognac region in Charente, France, while Armagnac comes from the Gascogne area of southern France. The classification system designating the number of years brandy has been aged, and its general quality, was created for cognac. V.O. (very old) is a good old brandy, and is an excellent choice for mixed drinks. V.S.O.P. (very special old pale) is a well-aged cognac that is better drunk straight than used in cocktails, where its special characteristics will likely be lost in the mixing. However, less expensive and less exceptional brandies from other areas in France, as well as other countries, have adopted this rating system, and those with the V.S.O.P. mark are good for blending into cocktails. X.O. (extra old) cognac should never be mixed with other ingredients.

Spain, Portugal and Italy make excellent brandies, usually with a more reasonable price tag. They are good choices for blender brandy drinks, as their generally more intense flavors will shine through. Good brandies from countries as far afield as Australia, South Africa and the North American wine-producing regions are also widely available. Greek brandy, such as Metaxa, is sweetened with caramel, so it is best to reduce the sugar or other sweet components in a cocktail if you use it.

BRANDY AND COGNAC RECIPES

Makes 1 serving

Essence of Apricot Martini

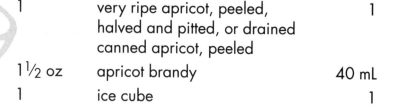

1	very ripe apricot, peeled, halved and pitted, or drained canned apricot, peeled	1
1½ oz	apricot brandy	40 mL
1	ice cube	1

1. In blender, on high speed, blend apricot, brandy and ice until smooth.

2. Pour into a martini glass.

Makes 1 serving

Cinnamon Apple

This festive-season drink will appeal to those who like their drinks not too sweet. For cinnamon lovers, garnish with a pinch of ground cinnamon.

½ cup	apple cider	125 mL
1 oz	brandy	25 mL
½ oz	cinnamon schnapps	15 mL
2	ice cubes	2

1. In blender, on high speed, blend apple cider, brandy, cinnamon schnapps and ice until smooth.

2. Pour into a wine glass.

Makes 1 serving

Rasp-Apple Cider

¼ cup	apple cider	50 mL
1 oz	apple brandy or brandy	25 mL
½ oz	raspberry liqueur or framboise	15 mL
½ oz	apple schnapps	15 mL
2	ice cubes	2
1	slice apple or fresh raspberry	1

1. In blender, on high speed, blend apple cider, brandy, raspberry liqueur, apple schnapps and ice until smooth.

2. Pour into a cocktail or martini glass and garnish with apple slice or raspberry.

Makes 1 serving

Yellow Cab

¼ cup	pineapple juice	50 mL
1 tbsp	freshly squeezed lime juice	15 mL
1 oz	cognac	25 mL
½ oz	vanilla vodka	15 mL
2	ice cubes	2
1	pineapple wedge or maraschino cherry	1

1. In blender, on high speed, blend pineapple juice, lime juice, cognac, vodka and ice until smooth.

2. Pour into an old-fashioned glass and garnish with pineapple wedge or cherry.

Makes 1 serving

Pineapple Brandy

¼ cup	pineapple juice	50 mL
½ tsp	grenadine	2 mL
1 oz	brandy	25 mL
½ oz	Galliano	15 mL
½ oz	orange liqueur	15 mL
2	ice cubes	2
1	twist orange rind	1

1. In blender, on high speed, blend pineapple juice, grenadine, brandy, Galliano, orange liqueur and ice until smooth.

2. Pour into an old-fashioned glass and garnish with orange twist.

Makes 1 serving

Peachy Keen

¼ cup	light (5%) cream	50 mL
¼ cup	frozen sliced peaches	50 mL
1½ oz	brandy	40 mL
½ oz	crème de cassis	15 mL
3	ice cubes	3
1	slice peach	1

1. In blender, on high speed, blend cream, frozen peaches, brandy, crème de cassis and ice until smooth.

2. Pour or strain through a fine sieve into a piña colada or old-fashioned glass and garnish with peach slice.

Makes 1 serving

TIP

Look for peach nectar or juice in bottles or cartons in the fruit juice section of well-stocked supermarkets and health food stores.

Raspy Peach

8	frozen raspberries	8
¼ cup	peach nectar or juice (see tip, at left)	50 mL
1 oz	brandy	25 mL
1 oz	raspberry liqueur or framboise	25 mL
1	ice cube	1
1	slice peach or fresh raspberry	1

1. In blender, on high speed, blend raspberries, peach nectar, brandy, raspberry liqueur and ice until smooth.

2. Pour into a cocktail or martini glass and garnish with peach slice or raspberry.

Makes 1 serving

TIP

Look for passion fruit nectar or juice in bottles or cartons in the fruit juice section of well-stocked supermarkets and health food stores.

Brandy Fruit Passion

½ cup	frozen sliced peaches	125 mL
¼ cup	apple cider or apple juice	50 mL
¼ cup	passion fruit nectar or juice (see tip, at left)	50 mL
1 tsp	chopped crystallized ginger	5 mL
1 oz	brandy	25 mL
1 oz	passion fruit liqueur	25 mL
2	ice cubes	2
1	slice peach	1

1. In blender, on high speed, blend frozen peaches, apple cider, passion fruit nectar, ginger, brandy, passion fruit liqueur and ice until smooth.

2. Pour into a highball glass and garnish with peach slice.

Makes 1 serving

Lichee Lust

4	canned lichees, drained	4
1 tbsp	syrup from canned lichees	15 mL
1 tsp	freshly squeezed lime juice	5 mL
1 oz	brandy	25 mL
2	ice cubes	2
Dash	grenadine	Dash

1. In blender, on high speed, blend lichees, syrup, lime juice, brandy and ice until smooth.

2. Pour into an old-fashioned glass and top with grenadine.

Makes 1 serving

Pom Pilot

1/4 cup	pomegranate seeds	50 mL
1 oz	orange liqueur	25 mL
1 oz	brandy	25 mL

1. In blender, on high speed, blend pomegranate seeds, orange liqueur and brandy until pomegranate flesh is separated from seed cores.

2. Strain through a fine sieve into an old-fashioned glass filled with ice.

Makes 1 serving

Sweet Canadian

Use a late-harvest dessert wine, such as Riesling or Vidal, for this classy sweet drink. You can rim the glass with maple sugar, if desired; wet the rim with either cognac or wine, or use lemon juice.

1 tsp	pure maple syrup	5 mL
½ tsp	freshly squeezed lemon juice	2 mL
1 oz	cognac or brandy	25 mL
1 oz	late-harvest white wine	25 mL
2	ice cubes	2

1. In blender, on high speed, blend maple syrup, lemon juice, cognac, wine and ice until smooth.

2. Pour into a martini glass.

Makes 1 serving

Peaches 'n' Cream

TIP

To peel a fresh peach, submerge it in boiling water for 10 to 15 seconds to loosen the skin. Or use drained canned peaches or frozen sliced peaches.

½ cup	cubed peeled peaches (see tip, at left)	125 mL
½ cup	half-and-half (10%) cream	125 mL
1 oz	brandy	25 mL
1 oz	peach schnapps	25 mL
2	ice cubes	2

1. In blender, on high speed, blend peaches, cream, brandy, peach schnapps and ice until smooth.

2. Pour into an old-fashioned glass.

Makes 1 serving

Peach Velvet

¼ cup	light (5%) cream	50 mL
2 oz	peach schnapps	50 mL
1 oz	brandy	25 mL
3	ice cubes	3
1	slice peach	1

1. In blender, on high speed, blend cream, peach schnapps, brandy and ice until smooth.

2. Pour into an old-fashioned glass and garnish with peach slice.

Makes 1 serving

Mango Velvet

If mangoes are in season, you can make this smooth mango drink with ⅓ cup (75 mL) chopped mango instead of the nectar and garnish with a slice of fresh mango.

¼ cup	mango nectar or juice (see tip, at left)	50 mL
2 tbsp	light (5%) cream	25 mL
1 oz	brandy	25 mL
1 oz	apricot brandy	25 mL
3	ice cubes	3
1	maraschino cherry (optional)	1

TIP

Look for mango nectar or juice in bottles or cartons in the fruit juice section of well-stocked supermarkets and health food stores.

1. In blender, on high speed, blend mango nectar, cream, brandy, apricot brandy and ice until smooth.

2. Pour into an old-fashioned glass and garnish with cherry, if desired.

Makes 1 serving

Easy Eggnog

This recipe contains a raw egg. If the food safety of raw eggs is a concern for you, use the pasteurized liquid whole egg instead.

1	egg yolk (or 2 tbsp/25 mL pasteurized liquid whole egg)	1
1/4 cup	whipping (35%) cream	50 mL
2 tsp	liquid honey	10 mL
2 oz	brandy or dark rum	50 mL
4	ice cubes	4
Pinch	freshly ground nutmeg	Pinch

1. In blender, on high speed, blend egg yolk, whipping cream, honey, brandy and ice until smooth.

2. Pour into an eggnog cup or a punch cup and sprinkle with nutmeg.

Makes 1 serving

Brandy Alexander

Despite the ice, this is a warming and rich winter cocktail.

3 tbsp	light (5%) cream	45 mL
1 oz	brandy	25 mL
1/2 oz	white crème de cacao	15 mL
1/2 oz	coffee liqueur	15 mL
3	ice cubes	3
Pinch	ground nutmeg	Pinch

1. In blender, on high speed, blend cream, brandy, crème de cacao, coffee liqueur and ice until smooth.

2. Pour into a martini glass and sprinkle with nutmeg.

Makes 1 serving

Polar Express

*For a petite
after-dinner treat
for 4, serve in small
chocolate cups.*

¼ cup	brewed espresso coffee, cooled	50 mL
2 tbsp	sweetened condensed milk	25 mL
1 oz	brandy	25 mL
½ oz	almond or hazelnut liqueur	15 mL
2	ice cubes	2

1. In blender, on high speed, blend coffee, condensed milk, brandy, almond liqueur and ice until smooth.

2. Pour into an old-fashioned glass.

Makes 1 serving

Purple Haze

*If you make this drink
during the summer,
garnish with a few
fresh black currants
or a blackberry.*

1 tbsp	black currant cordial	15 mL
1½ oz	brandy	40 mL
½ oz	crème de cassis	15 mL
2	ice cubes	2

1. In blender, on high speed, blend black currant cordial, brandy, crème de cassis and ice until smooth.

2. Pour into a martini glass.

Apricot Fizz

This cocktail, combining the flavors of orange and apricot, has a touch of tang and a bit of fizz.

2 tbsp	freshly squeezed orange juice	25 mL
1 tbsp	freshly squeezed lemon juice	15 mL
1 ½ oz	apricot brandy	40 mL
3	ice cubes	3
¼ cup	chilled club soda	50 mL
1	twist orange rind or slice lemon	1

1. In blender, on high speed, blend orange juice, lemon juice, brandy and ice until smooth and frothy.

2. Pour into a wine glass and top with club soda. Garnish with orange twist or lemon slice.

Brandy Fizz

This recipe contains a raw egg white. If the food safety of raw eggs is a concern for you, use the pasteurized liquid egg white instead.

1	egg white (or 2 tbsp/25 mL pasteurized liquid egg white)	1
2 tbsp	freshly squeezed lemon juice	25 mL
2 tsp	confectioner's (icing) sugar	10 mL
2 oz	brandy	50 mL
2	ice cubes	2
2 tbsp	soda water or seltzer (approx.)	25 mL

1. In blender, on high speed, blend egg white, lemon juice, sugar, brandy and ice until smooth and frothy.

2. Pour into a highball glass and top with soda.

Frozen Scorpion

3	ice cubes	3
2 tbsp	frozen orange juice concentrate	25 mL
4 tsp	freshly squeezed lime juice	20 mL
1 tsp	confectioner's (icing) sugar	5 mL
3	drops almond extract	3
1 oz	cognac or other brandy	25 mL
1 oz	amber rum	25 mL

1. In blender, pulse ice until crushed. On high speed, blend in orange juice concentrate, lime juice, sugar, almond extract, cognac and rum until slushy.

2. Pour into an old-fashioned glass.

TIP

Look for peach nectar or juice in bottles or cartons in the fruit juice section of well-stocked supermarkets and health food stores.

Lazy Hazy Sunday

¼ cup	peach nectar or juice (see tip, at left)	50 mL
¼ cup	white grape juice	50 mL
2 tbsp	frozen orange juice concentrate	25 mL
1½ oz	peach brandy	40 mL
2	ice cubes	2
3	grapes, skewered	3

1. In blender, on high speed, blend peach nectar, grape juice, orange juice concentrate, brandy and ice until smooth.

2. Pour into a piña colada glass and garnish with skewered grapes.

Makes 1 serving

Instead of the cranberries, garnish this elegant drink with a slice of lime or a twist of lime rind.

Cognac Cosmo

2 tbsp	frozen limeade concentrate	25 mL
2 tbsp	cranberry juice	25 mL
1 oz	cognac	25 mL
1 oz	vodka	25 mL
1	ice cube	1
3	frozen or fresh cranberries	3

1. In blender, on high speed, blend limeade concentrate, cranberry juice, cognac, vodka and ice until smooth.

2. Pour into a martini glass and garnish with cranberries.

Makes 1 serving

Maple Orange Frappé

1/2 cup	orange sorbet	125 mL
1/3 cup	freshly squeezed orange juice	75 mL
2 tsp	pure maple syrup	10 mL
1 oz	brandy	25 mL
1 oz	orange liqueur	25 mL
2	ice cubes	2
1	slice orange or twist orange rind	1

1. In blender, on high speed, blend sorbet, orange juice, maple syrup, brandy, orange liqueur and ice until smooth.

2. Pour into a piña colada or old-fashioned glass and garnish with orange slice or twist.

Makes 1 serving

Sunny Sunrise

Garnish this sunny drink with a slice of orange, skewered cubed mango, a kumquat or a cape gooseberry.

¼ cup	orange sorbet	50 mL
¼ cup	mango nectar or juice (see tip, page 14)	50 mL
1 oz	brandy	25 mL
1 oz	almond liqueur	25 mL

1. In blender, on high speed, blend sorbet, mango nectar, brandy and almond liqueur until smooth.

2. Pour into a piña colada or old-fashioned glass.

Makes 1 serving

Apple Crisp

¼ cup	vanilla ice cream	50 mL
1 oz	apple brandy	25 mL
½ oz	Irish cream liqueur	15 mL
1	cinnamon stick (or pinch ground cinnamon)	1

1. In blender, on high speed, blend ice cream, brandy and Irish cream liqueur until smooth.

2. Pour into a martini glass and garnish with cinnamon.

This drink has all the aroma and flavors of a beautiful autumn day.

Apple, Date and Nut Smoothie

½ cup	vanilla ice cream	125 mL
¼ cup	apple cider or apple juice	50 mL
2	chopped pitted dates	2
1 oz	apple brandy or brandy	25 mL
1 oz	almond liqueur	25 mL
2	ice cubes	2
Pinch	ground nutmeg	Pinch
1	slice apple	1

1. In blender, on high speed, blend ice cream, apple cider, dates, brandy, almond liqueur and ice until smooth.

2. Pour into a highball glass and sprinkle with nutmeg. Garnish with apple slice.

For a smoother version of this creamy purple-hued drink, strain through a fine sieve. If you wish, you can replace the banana garnish with a few blueberries.

Banana-Berry

½	frozen ripe banana	½
½ cup	vanilla ice cream	125 mL
¼ cup	plain or blueberry-flavored yogurt	50 mL
¼ cup	frozen blueberries	50 mL
1 oz	brandy	25 mL
½ oz	crème de banane	15 mL
1	slice banana	1

1. In blender, on high speed, blend frozen banana, ice cream, yogurt, blueberries, brandy and crème de banane until smooth.

2. Pour into an old-fashioned glass and garnish with banana slice.

Cherry Pie

Frothy and a lovely shade of pink, this cherry-piqued drink will satisfy dessert and cocktail cravings in one glass.

TIP

Cherry brandy and kirsch (or *kirschwasser*) shouldn't be confused. Cherry brandy is a brandy (or sometimes another liquor) flavored and sweetened with cherries, while kirsch is an eau de vie distilled from the cherries themselves.

¼ cup	vanilla ice cream	50 mL
1 oz	cherry brandy	25 mL
1 oz	white crème de cacao	25 mL
½ oz	kirsch	15 mL
1	ice cube	1
	Grated semisweet chocolate (optional)	

1. In blender, on high speed, blend ice cream, brandy, crème de cacao, kirsch and ice until smooth.

2. Pour into a martini or wine glass and garnish with chocolate, if desired.

Hint o' Raspberry Cream

¼ cup	vanilla ice cream	50 mL
2 tbsp	light (5%) cream	25 mL
1 ½ oz	brandy	40 mL
½ oz	raspberry liqueur or framboise	15 mL
3	fresh raspberries	3

1. In blender, on high speed, blend ice cream, cream, brandy and raspberry liqueur until smooth.

2. Pour into a piña colada or old-fashioned glass. Skewer the raspberries on a cocktail stick and place in drink.

Makes 1 serving

Peach Dream

2 tbsp	vanilla ice cream	25 mL
2 tbsp	orange juice	25 mL
1 oz	peach brandy	25 mL
1 oz	Galliano	25 mL
1	ice cube	1
1	slice peach (optional)	1

1. In blender, on high speed, blend ice cream, orange juice, brandy, Galliano and ice until smooth.

2. Pour into a martini glass and garnish with peach slice, if desired.

Makes 1 serving

Creamsicle

¼ cup	vanilla ice cream	50 mL
¼ cup	freshly squeezed orange juice	50 mL
1 oz	cognac	25 mL
1 oz	vanilla vodka	25 mL
1	slice orange	1

1. In blender, on high speed, blend ice cream, orange juice, cognac and vodka until smooth.

2. Pour into an old-fashioned glass and garnish with orange slice.

Cherry Cheesecake

For extra fun, garnish this creamy dessert drink with a fresh cherry and a sprinkle of fresh graham cracker crumbs.

10	frozen pitted sweet cherries	10
3 tbsp	vanilla or cherry ice cream	45 mL
1 tbsp	mascarpone or cream cheese	15 mL
1½ oz	cherry brandy	40 mL
½ oz	almond liqueur	15 mL

1. In blender, on high speed, blend cherries, ice cream, mascarpone, brandy and almond liqueur until smooth.

2. Pour into an old-fashioned glass.

Chocolate-Cherry Chiller

½ cup	chocolate milk	125 mL
½ cup	chocolate ice cream	125 mL
¼ cup	frozen or canned pitted sweet cherries	50 mL
1 oz	brandy	25 mL
1 oz	kirsch	25 mL
1	fresh cherry (optional)	1
	Grated semisweet chocolate (optional)	

1. In blender, on high speed, blend chocolate milk, ice cream, frozen cherries, brandy and kirsch until smooth.

2. Pour into an old-fashioned glass and garnish with cherry and/or chocolate.

Choco-Blaster

Mmmm… rich chocolate in a glass. You can add a splash of color by garnishing the rim of the glass with a strawberry.

¾ cup	chocolate ice cream	175 mL
¾ cup	chocolate milk	175 mL
1 oz	brandy	25 mL
1 oz	white crème de cacao	25 mL
	Grated semisweet chocolate	

1. In blender, on high speed, blend ice cream, chocolate milk, brandy and crème de cacao until smooth.

2. Pour into a piña colada or old-fashioned glass and garnish with chocolate.

Mary's Milkshake

⅓ cup	vanilla ice cream	75 mL
2 tbsp	milk	25 mL
2 oz	brandy	50 mL
¾ oz	crème de cacao	22 mL

1. In blender, on high speed, blend ice cream, milk and brandy until smooth.

2. Pour into an old-fashioned glass and drizzle with crème de cacao.

Iced Mint Brandy

You can serve this festive minty drink as an aperitif, like an eggnog, or as dessert. At Christmastime, garnish with a small peppermint candy cane or rim the glass with red-tinted sugar, which is available at cake-decorating supply stores.

3 tbsp	vanilla ice cream	45 mL
1 oz	brandy	25 mL
1/2 oz	white crème de cacao	15 mL
1/2 oz	white crème de menthe	15 mL

1. In blender, on high speed, blend ice cream, brandy, crème de cacao and crème de menthe until smooth.

2. Pour into a martini glass.

Cherry Cola

1/4 cup	vanilla ice cream	50 mL
1/4 cup	cherry-flavored or plain yogurt	50 mL
1/4 cup	frozen pitted sweet cherries	50 mL
1/4 cup	chilled cola	50 mL
2 oz	cherry brandy	50 mL
1	maraschino cherry	1

1. In blender, on high speed, blend ice cream, yogurt, frozen cherries, cola and brandy until smooth.

2. Pour into a highball glass and garnish with cherry.

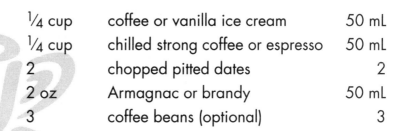

Makes 1 serving

Coffee-Date Smoothie

¼ cup	coffee or vanilla ice cream	50 mL
¼ cup	chilled strong coffee or espresso	50 mL
2	chopped pitted dates	2
2 oz	Armagnac or brandy	50 mL
3	coffee beans (optional)	3

1. In blender, on high speed, blend ice cream, coffee, dates and Armagnac until smooth.

2. Pour into an old-fashioned glass and garnish with coffee beans, if desired.

Makes 1 serving

The Capital "S"

This fabulous dessert drink features the classic French combination of Armagnac and prunes (the equivalent of North America's rum and raisin).

¼ cup	vanilla ice cream	50 mL
2	pitted prunes	2
2 oz	Armagnac	50 mL

1. In blender, on high speed, blend ice cream, prunes and Armagnac until prunes are very finely chopped but not puréed.

2. Pour into an old-fashioned glass.

vodka

V ODKA IS A CLEAR SPIRIT distilled from a grain such as rye, wheat or barley, potatoes or even beets. The name "vodka" is the Russian diminutive of water, *voda*, literally "little water," but its function in blender cocktails is anything but small. Vodka originated in the northeastern regions of Europe, with Russia, Poland and Ukraine all claiming to be the original makers of the spirit. Vodka is filtered through charcoal to give it smoothness and remove almost all traces of flavor, making it a superb spirit for mixed drinks. Vodka enhances and gives heft to the flavors of the other ingredients in a cocktail, making it the ideal mixer.

Despite all the effort to make vodkas as smooth and tasteless as possible, each brand of vodka has its own definite characteristics, however subtle. Blind tastings by experts almost inevitably upset previous tastings, so when it comes to smoothness, hints of flavor and aroma, we suggest you trust your own senses and choose a brand of vodka that appeals the most to your taste. Some premium brands are frightfully expensive, and whatever makes them special when imbibed straight will probably disappear when a drink is mixed. Keep your vodka in the freezer, as very cold vodka always feels the smoothest on the palate.

Vodka takes very well to flavoring, and flavored brands such as vanilla vodka, raspberry vodka, pepper vodka and many others allow the cocktail maker a plethora of tastes with which to experiment.

VODKA RECIPES

continued next page…

A delightfully ambiguous drink for indecisive imbibers.

Apples or Oranges Martini

2 tbsp	orange sorbet	25 mL
2 tbsp	apple cider or apple juice	25 mL
1 oz	apple vodka	25 mL
1 oz	orange liqueur	25 mL
1	thin slice orange	1
1	slice apple	1

1. In blender, on high speed, blend sorbet, apple cider, vodka and orange liqueur until smooth.

2. Pour into a martini glass and garnish with orange and apple slices.

Candied Apple Martini

1 oz	apple vodka	25 mL
1 oz	apple brandy	25 mL
½ oz	raspberry liqueur or framboise	15 mL
2	ice cubes	2
1	slice apple (optional)	1
3	fresh raspberries (optional)	3

1. In blender, on high speed, blend vodka, brandy, raspberry liqueur and ice until smooth.

2. Pour into a martini glass and garnish with apple slice and/or raspberries.

Makes 1 serving

Cinnamon Appletini

TIP

To make this drink with vodka instead of apple vodka, decrease the white cranberry juice by half and add 2 tbsp (25 mL) apple cider or apple juice or 2 tsp (10 mL) frozen apple juice concentrate and 1 tbsp (15 mL) water.

1/4 cup	white cranberry juice	50 mL
1 oz	apple vodka (see tip, at left)	25 mL
1/2 oz	cinnamon schnapps	15 mL
2	ice cubes	2
1	cinnamon stick or slice green apple	1

1. In blender, on high speed, blend cranberry juice, vodka, cinnamon schnapps and ice until smooth.

2. Pour into a large martini or wine glass and garnish with cinnamon stick or apple slice.

Makes 1 serving

Pink Grapefruitini

1/4 cup	pink grapefruit juice	50 mL
1 tbsp	freshly squeezed lime juice	15 mL
1 tbsp	Simple Syrup (see page 5)	15 mL
1 1/2 oz	vodka or citrus vodka	40 mL
2	ice cubes	2
1	twist orange or lime rind	1

1. In blender, on high speed, blend grapefruit juice, lime juice, Simple Syrup, vodka and ice until smooth.

2. Pour into a martini glass and garnish with orange or lime twist.

Cran-Orangetini

If you don't have cranberry vodka on hand, use an equal amount of regular vodka and add 1 tbsp (15 mL) cranberry juice or 1 tsp (5 mL) cranberry juice concentrate.

1 ½ oz	cranberry vodka (see tip, at left)	40 mL
1 oz	orange liqueur	25 mL
2	ice cubes	2
1	twist orange rind	1

1. In blender, on high speed, blend vodka, orange liqueur and ice until smooth.

2. Pour into a martini glass and garnish with orange twist.

French Martini

This elegant, fruity martini has a lovely purple-golden hue, like a sunset in Paris.

6	frozen raspberries	6
2 tbsp	frozen pineapple juice concentrate	25 mL
1 ½ oz	raspberry vodka or vodka	40 mL
½ oz	raspberry liqueur or framboise	15 mL
1	ice cube	1
3	fresh raspberries	3

1. In blender, on high speed, blend frozen raspberries, pineapple juice concentrate, vodka, raspberry liqueur and ice until smooth.

2. Pour or strain through a fine sieve into a martini glass and garnish with raspberries.

Makes 1 serving

Pineapple-Raspberry Martini

¼ cup	pineapple juice	50 mL
2 oz	vodka	50 mL
½ oz	raspberry liqueur or framboise	15 mL
2	ice cubes	2
3	fresh raspberries	3

1. In blender, on high speed, blend pineapple juice, vodka, raspberry liqueur and ice until smooth.

2. Pour into a large martini or wine glass and garnish with raspberries.

Makes 1 serving

Strawberry Pepper Martini

6	frozen strawberries	6
6	whole black peppercorns	6
3 oz	vodka	75 mL
Dash	orange liqueur	Dash

1. In blender, on high speed, blend strawberries, peppercorns, vodka and orange liqueur until strawberries are puréed and peppercorns are coarsely crushed.

2. Pour into a martini glass.

Strawberry Basiltini

You can change this intriguing drink into a Strawberry Mintini by replacing the fresh basil with fresh mint.

4	frozen strawberries	4
3 tbsp	frozen cranberry juice concentrate	45 mL
1 tbsp	chopped fresh basil	15 mL
Pinch	cracked black pepper	Pinch
1 oz	strawberry vodka or vodka	25 mL
½ oz	orange liqueur	15 mL
½ oz	raspberry liqueur or framboise	15 mL
2	ice cubes	2
1	fresh basil leaf	1

1. In blender, on high speed, blend strawberries, cranberry juice concentrate, chopped basil, pepper, vodka, orange liqueur, raspberry liqueur and ice until smooth.

2. Strain through a fine sieve into a large martini or cocktail glass and garnish with basil leaf.

Watermelon Martini

A small pinch of salt intensifies the watermelon flavor.

⅓ cup	cubed seedless watermelon, chilled	75 mL
Pinch	salt	Pinch
2 oz	vodka or gin	50 mL
1	ice cube	1

1. In blender, on high speed, blend watermelon, salt, vodka and ice until smooth.

2. Pour into a martini glass.

Makes 1 serving

Fruit Exotini

Garnish this exotic fruit drink with a slice of pear, a fresh or drained canned lichee, a dusting of cardamom or a twist of lemon rind.

TIP

Look for pear nectar or juice in bottles or cartons in the fruit juice section of well-stocked supermarkets and health food stores.

¼ cup	pear nectar or juice (see tip, at left)	50 mL
1 tbsp	freshly squeezed lemon juice	15 mL
Pinch	ground cardamom	Pinch
1 oz	vodka	25 mL
1 oz	pear liqueur or pear eau de vie, such as Poire William	25 mL
½ oz	lichee liqueur	15 mL
2	ice cubes	2

1. In blender, on high speed, blend pear nectar, lemon juice, cardamom, vodka, pear liqueur, lichee liqueur and ice until smooth.

2. Pour into a large martini or cocktail glass.

Makes 1 serving

Tutti-Frutti Martini

2 tbsp	unsweetened apple juice	25 mL
2 tbsp	unsweetened pineapple juice	25 mL
1 ½ tsp	freshly squeezed lime juice	7 mL
1 ½ oz	raspberry vodka or citrus vodka	40 mL
½ oz	melon liqueur	25 mL
½ oz	peach schnapps	25 mL
1	ice cube	1
1	small wedge fresh pineapple, apple, peach or lime	1

1. In blender, on high speed, blend apple, pineapple and lime juices, vodka, melon liqueur, peach schnapps and ice until smooth.

2. Pour into a martini glass and garnish with fruit.

Nutty Cream Martini

2 tbsp	vanilla ice cream	25 mL
2 oz	vodka	50 mL
1 oz	almond or hazelnut liqueur	25 mL
1	ice cube	1

1. In blender, on high speed, blend ice cream, vodka, almond liqueur and ice until smooth.

2. Pour into a martini glass or a wide-mouthed champagne glass.

Vanilla Vanilla Cream Martini

2 tbsp	vanilla ice cream	25 mL
2½ oz	vanilla vodka	65 mL
½ oz	orange liqueur	15 mL
1	ice cube	1
1	small piece vanilla bean	1

1. In blender, on high speed, blend ice cream, vodka, orange liqueur and ice until smooth.

2. Pour into a martini glass and garnish with vanilla bean.

Makes 1 serving

Lemongrass Martini

2 tbsp	chopped lemongrass (white part only)	25 mL
2 oz	vodka	50 mL
1 oz	dry white vermouth	25 mL
1	ice cube	1

1. In blender, on high speed, blend lemongrass, vodka, vermouth and ice until lemongrass is very finely chopped.

2. Strain through a fine sieve into a martini glass.

Makes 1 serving

Ginger Carrottini

1	small carrot, peeled and chopped	1
1 tsp	grated gingerroot	5 mL
2 oz	vodka	50 mL
1 oz	dry white vermouth	25 mL
2	ice cubes	2

1. In blender, on high speed, blend carrot, ginger, vodka, vermouth and ice until carrot is very finely chopped.

2. Strain through a fine sieve into a martini glass.

Frozen Cosmo

Sweeter than a regular cosmo, but balanced with lime juice, this is a refreshing summer cocktail.

3	ice cubes	3
1 tbsp	frozen cranberry cocktail concentrate	15 mL
2 tsp	freshly squeezed lime juice	10 mL
2 oz	vodka	50 mL
1 oz	orange brandy or orange liqueur	25 mL
1 to 3	frozen cranberries (optional)	1 to 3

1. In blender, pulse ice until crushed. On high speed, blend in cranberry cocktail concentrate, lime juice, vodka and orange brandy until slushy.

2. Pour into a martini glass and garnish with frozen cranberries, if desired.

Watermelon Cosmo

1 cup	frozen cubed seedless watermelon	250 mL
2 tbsp	cranberry cocktail	25 mL
4 tsp	freshly squeezed lime juice	20 mL
1½ oz	vodka or citrus vodka	40 mL
½ oz	melon liqueur	15 mL
2 dashes	angostura bitters	2 dashes

1. In blender, on high speed, blend watermelon, cranberry cocktail, lime juice, vodka, melon liqueur and bitters until smooth.

2. Strain through a fine sieve into a martini glass.

Makes 1 serving

Breezy Sea

¼ cup	grapefruit juice	50 mL
¼ cup	cranberry juice	50 mL
1 ½ oz	citrus vodka or vodka	40 mL
2	ice cubes	2
3	frozen cranberries (or 1 twist lemon rind)	3

1. In blender, on high speed, blend grapefruit juice, cranberry juice, vodka and ice until smooth.

2. Pour into a piña colada or old-fashioned glass and garnish with cranberries (or lemon twist).

Makes 1 serving

Gout Potion

Cherries are known for their gout-preventive properties. But everyone will enjoy this cocktail, not just those who suffer from gout.

¼ cup	drained canned sweet or sour cherries	50 mL
¼ cup	sweet or sour cherry juice or cranberry cocktail	50 mL
2 oz	vodka	50 mL
4	ice cubes	4

1. In blender, on high speed, blend cherries, cherry juice, vodka and ice until smooth.

2. Pour into an old-fashioned glass.

Makes 1 serving

Cherry-Orange Blast

Garnish this plum-colored delight with a cherry or a twist of orange rind.

2	ice cubes	2
3 tbsp	orange juice	45 mL
1 oz	vanilla vodka or vodka	25 mL
1 oz	cherry brandy	25 mL
Splash	dry vermouth	Splash

1. In blender, pulse ice until crushed. On high speed, blend in orange juice, vodka, cherry brandy and vermouth until smooth.

2. Pour into a martini glass.

Makes 1 serving

Furry Collar

1/4 cup	orange juice	50 mL
1 1/2 oz	vanilla vodka	40 mL
1 oz	apricot brandy	25 mL
2	ice cubes	2
1	twist orange rind or slice orange	1

1. In blender, on high speed, blend orange juice, vodka, apricot brandy and ice until smooth.

2. Pour into a martini or wine glass and garnish with orange.

The Head Spinner

1 tbsp	freshly squeezed lime juice	15 mL
½ oz	currant vodka or vodka	15 mL
½ oz	white or amber rum	15 mL
½ oz	gin	15 mL
½ oz	orange liqueur	15 mL
½ oz	raspberry liqueur or framboise	15 mL
3	ice cubes	3
¼ cup	chilled lemon-lime soda	50 mL
3	raspberries, skewered	3
1	slice lime	1

1. In blender, on high speed, blend lime juice, vodka, rum, gin, orange liqueur, raspberry liqueur and ice until smooth.

2. Pour into an old-fashioned glass and top with lemon-lime soda. Garnish with skewered raspberries and lime slice.

Peach Melba

The kirsch adds a sophisticated touch to this beautiful orange- and red-hued drink. During peach season, garnish with a slice of fresh peach.

1 cup	frozen sliced peaches	250 mL
¾ cup	raspberry juice	175 mL
1½ oz	raspberry vodka or vodka	40 mL
½ oz	kirsch	15 mL

1. In blender, on high speed, blend peaches, raspberry juice, vodka and kirsch until slushy.

2. Pour into an old-fashioned glass.

Festive Spiced Pear

Makes 1 serving

TIP

Look for pear nectar or juice in bottles or cartons in the fruit juice section of well-stocked supermarkets and health food stores.

3 tbsp	pear nectar or juice (see tip, at left)	45 mL
1 tbsp	freshly squeezed lemon juice	15 mL
1 oz	vodka or vanilla vodka	25 mL
½ oz	orange liqueur	15 mL
Pinch	ground cardamom or cinnamon	Pinch
2	ice cubes	2
1	slice pear	1

1. In blender, on high speed, blend pear nectar, lemon juice, vodka, orange liqueur, cardamom and ice until smooth.

2. Pour into a cocktail or old-fashioned glass and garnish with pear slice.

Raspberry Sensation

Makes 1 serving

¾ cup	frozen raspberries	175 mL
½ cup	raspberry juice	125 mL
2 tbsp	freshly squeezed lemon juice	25 mL
1 tbsp	Simple Syrup (see page 5)	15 mL
2 oz	raspberry vodka or vodka	50 mL
1	ice cube	1
1	twist lemon rind or slice lemon	1

1. In blender, on high speed, blend raspberries, raspberry juice, lemon juice, Simple Syrup, vodka and ice until smooth.

2. Pour into a wine glass and garnish with lemon.

Makes 1 serving

Raspberry-Nut

1 ½ oz	raspberry vodka	40 mL
1 oz	hazelnut liqueur	25 mL
2	ice cubes	2

1. In blender, on high speed, blend vodka, hazelnut liqueur and ice until smooth.

2. Pour into a martini glass.

Makes 1 serving

Cran-Raspberry Creation

½ cup	cranberry-raspberry juice	125 mL
1 oz	currant vodka or vodka	25 mL
½ oz	raspberry liqueur or framboise	15 mL
2	ice cubes	2
3	fresh raspberries or frozen cranberries	3

1. In blender, on high speed, blend cranberry-raspberry juice, vodka, raspberry liqueur and ice until smooth.

2. Pour into a martini glass and garnish with raspberries or cranberries.

Makes 1 serving

Pink Berries

½ cup	cranberry-raspberry juice	125 mL
6	frozen strawberries	6
1 ½ oz	strawberry vodka or vodka	40 mL
½ oz	raspberry liqueur or framboise	15 mL
3	frozen cranberries or fresh raspberries (or 1 fresh strawberry)	3

1. In blender, on high speed, blend cranberry-raspberry juice, frozen strawberries, vodka and raspberry liqueur until smooth.

2. Pour into a piña colada or old-fashioned glass and garnish with cranberries or raspberries (or strawberry).

Makes 1 serving

Frozen Rush Hour

1 ½ tsp	black currant concentrate (such as Ribena)	7 mL
1 oz	vodka	25 mL
1 oz	red vermouth	25 mL
¼ oz	cherry brandy	7 mL
2	ice cubes	2

1. In blender, on high speed, blend black currant concentrate, vodka, vermouth, cherry brandy and ice until smooth.

2. Pour into an old-fashioned or martini glass.

Makes 1 serving

Hot Honeydew Freezie

You can omit the hot peppers if you use chili pepper vodka instead of regular vodka. Hot pepper lovers should use both.

1 cup	cubed very ripe honeydew melon	250 mL
2 tbsp	freshly squeezed lime juice	25 mL
1 ½ tsp	confectioner's (icing) sugar	7 mL
1 tsp	chopped seeded green hot pepper	5 mL
Pinch	salt	Pinch
1 ½ oz	vodka or chili pepper vodka	40 mL
½ oz	orange liqueur	15 mL
6	ice cubes	6

1. In blender, on high speed, blend melon, lime juice, sugar, hot pepper, salt, vodka, orange liqueur and ice until smooth.

2. Pour into a highball or large stemmed punch glass.

Makes 1 serving

Hot Watermelon Freezie

1 cup	cubed seedless watermelon	250 mL
1 tbsp	freshly squeezed lemon juice	25 mL
1 tsp	confectioner's (icing) sugar	5 mL
1 tsp	chopped seeded red hot pepper	5 mL
Pinch	salt	Pinch
1 ½ oz	vodka or chili pepper vodka	40 mL
½ oz	orange liqueur	15 mL
6	ice cubes	6

1. In blender, on high speed, blend melon, lemon juice, sugar, hot pepper, salt, vodka, orange liqueur and ice until smooth.

2. Pour into a highball or large stemmed punch glass.

Makes 1 serving

Watermelon and Strawberry Slushy

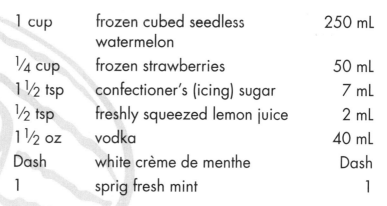

1 cup	frozen cubed seedless watermelon	250 mL
¼ cup	frozen strawberries	50 mL
1 ½ tsp	confectioner's (icing) sugar	7 mL
½ tsp	freshly squeezed lemon juice	2 mL
1 ½ oz	vodka	40 mL
Dash	white crème de menthe	Dash
1	sprig fresh mint	1

1. In blender, on high speed, blend watermelon, strawberries, sugar, lemon juice, vodka and crème de menthe until smooth.

2. Pour into an old-fashioned glass and garnish with mint.

Makes 1 serving

TIP

If you can't find strawberry or watermelon vodka, use an equal amount of regular vodka and garnish with 3 fresh strawberries or 1 wedge watermelon.

Meloncholy

1 ½ oz	strawberry or watermelon vodka (see tip, at left)	40 mL
1 oz	melon liqueur	25 mL
2	ice cubes	2
1	honeydew or watermelon ball, skewered, or fresh strawberry	1

1. In blender, on high speed, blend vodka, melon liqueur and ice until smooth.

2. Pour into a martini glass and garnish with skewered melon ball or strawberry.

Melon Twister

Makes 1 serving

¾ cup	cranberry juice	175 mL
1 oz	watermelon vodka or vodka	25 mL
½ oz	melon liqueur	15 mL
3	ice cubes	3
1	honeydew melon ball, skewered, or slice lime or orange	1

1. In blender, on high speed, blend cranberry juice, vodka, melon liqueur and ice until smooth.

2. Pour into an old-fashioned glass and garnish with skewered melon ball or citrus slice.

Chi-Chi

Makes 1 serving

Invite the taste of the tropics in on a summer day with this cousin of a piña colada.

¼ cup	pineapple juice	50 mL
3 tbsp	creamed coconut	45 mL
1 tbsp	frozen orange juice concentrate	15 mL
1 oz	vodka	25 mL
½ oz	coconut or spiced rum	15 mL
3	ice cubes	3
1	slice orange	1
1	maraschino cherry	1

1. In blender, on high speed, blend pineapple juice, creamed coconut, orange juice concentrate, vodka, rum and ice until smooth.

2. Pour into a piña colada glass and garnish with orange slice and cherry.

Brandy Alexander (page 15)

Overleaf: Maple Orange Frappé (page 19)

Makes 1 serving

Nutty Chi-Chi

¼ cup	pineapple juice	50 mL
2 tbsp	creamed coconut	25 mL
1 tbsp	frozen orange juice concentrate	15 mL
1 oz	vodka or vanilla vodka	25 mL
1 oz	almond liqueur	25 mL
3	ice cubes	3
1	slice orange	1
1	maraschino cherry	1

1. In blender, on high speed, blend pineapple juice, creamed coconut, orange juice concentrate, vodka, almond liqueur and ice until smooth.

2. Pour into a piña colada glass and garnish with orange slice and cherry.

Makes 1 serving

Mama's Mango

½	mango, peeled and cubed	½
1 tbsp	freshly squeezed lime juice	15 mL
1 tsp	confectioner's (icing) sugar	5 mL
1 oz	vodka	25 mL
½ oz	orange liqueur	15 mL
4	ice cubes	4

1. In blender, on high speed, blend mango, lime juice, sugar, vodka, orange liqueur and ice until smooth.

2. Pour into an old-fashioned or large stemmed punch glass.

Overleaf: The Fizzmopolitan (page 66)

Barbecued Caesar (page 57)

Fruit Explosion

Makes 1 serving

TIP

Look for passion fruit nectar or juice and mango nectar or juice in bottles or cartons in the fruit juice section of well-stocked supermarkets and health food stores.

¼ cup	passion fruit nectar or juice (see tip, at left)	50 mL
¼ cup	mango nectar or juice (see tip, at left)	50 mL
2 tbsp	frozen cranberry juice concentrate	25 mL
1½ oz	watermelon or strawberry vodka	40 mL
2	ice cubes	2
1	strawberry or maraschino cherry	1

1. In blender, on high speed, blend passion fruit nectar, mango nectar, cranberry juice concentrate, vodka and ice until smooth.

2. Pour into a piña colada or highball glass and garnish with strawberry.

Snowy Gold

Makes 1 serving

¼ cup	white cranberry juice	50 mL
1 oz	vodka	25 mL
1 oz	passion fruit liqueur	25 mL
2	ice cubes	2
	Few slices red or green grape	

1. In blender, on high speed, blend cranberry juice, vodka, passion fruit liqueur and ice until smooth.

2. Pour into a martini glass and garnish with grape slices.

Makes 1 serving

Guavalicious

TIP

Look for guava nectar
or juice in bottles or
cartons in the fruit
juice section of well-
stocked supermarkets
and health food stores.

¼ cup	pineapple juice	50 mL
¼ cup	guava nectar or juice (see tip, at left)	50 mL
1 oz	watermelon vodka or vodka	25 mL
1 oz	passion fruit liqueur	25 mL
Dash	angostura bitters	Dash
3	ice cubes	3
1	maraschino cherry	1
1	pineapple wedge	1

1. In blender, on high speed, blend pineapple juice, guava nectar, vodka, passion fruit liqueur, bitters and ice until smooth.

2. Pour into a piña colada glass. Skewer cherry and pineapple and garnish drink.

Makes 1 serving

Pom-Pom

¼ cup	pomegranate seeds	50 mL
¼ cup	orange juice	50 mL
1 tsp	freshly squeezed lemon juice	5 mL
½ tsp	confectioner's (icing) sugar	2 mL
1½ oz	vodka	40 mL

1. In blender, on high speed, blend pomegranate seeds, orange and lemon juices, sugar and vodka until pomegranate flesh is separated from seed cores.

2. Strain through a fine sieve into a highball glass filled with ice.

Makes 1 serving

TIP

Pomegranate cocktails can be made with purchased pomegranate juice or with freshly squeezed juice. To juice a pomegranate, cut it in half and use a citrus reamer or juicer; strain. One large pomegranate will yield about 1/2 cup (125 mL) juice.

Pom Vodka Julep

1/4 cup	pomegranate juice (see tip, at left)	50 mL
2 tbsp	grapefruit juice	25 mL
1 tbsp	freshly squeezed lime juice	15 mL
1 tbsp	Simple Syrup (see page 5)	15 mL
1 tbsp	chopped fresh mint	15 mL
1 1/2 oz	vodka	40 mL
3	ice cubes	3
1	sprig fresh mint	1

1. In blender, on high speed, blend pomegranate juice, grapefruit juice, lime juice, Simple Syrup, chopped mint, vodka and ice until smooth.

2. Pour into an old-fashioned glass and garnish with mint sprig.

Makes 1 serving

If you love pomegranates, you'll love this cocktail!

Pomegranate Cocktail

1/4 cup	pomegranate seeds	50 mL
1 tsp	freshly squeezed lime juice	5 mL
1/2 tsp	confectioner's (icing) sugar	2 mL
1 oz	vodka	25 mL

1. In blender, on high speed, blend pomegranate seeds, lime juice, sugar and vodka until pomegranate flesh is separated from seed cores.

2. Strain through a fine sieve into an old-fashioned glass filled with ice.

Makes 1 serving

Sweet Sunburst

TIP

Look for pomegranate-cherry juice in bottles or cartons in the fruit juice section of well-stocked supermarkets and health food stores.

¼ cup	pomegranate-cherry juice (see tip, at left)	50 mL
1 oz	late-harvest white dessert wine or Sauternes	25 mL
½ oz	citrus vodka or vodka	15 mL
2	ice cubes	2
1 tsp	fresh pomegranate seeds (optional)	5 mL

1. In blender, on high speed, blend pomegranate-cherry juice, wine, vodka and ice until smooth.

2. Pour into a martini glass and garnish with pomegranate seeds, if desired.

Makes 1 serving

Gypsy Rose

Use only unsprayed, fragrant rose petals.

TIP

If rose petals are not available, substitute ¼ tsp (1 mL) rosewater (no need to strain).

¼ cup	loosely packed rose petals	50 mL
2 oz	vodka	50 mL
1 tsp	grenadine	5 mL
2	ice cubes	2

1. In blender, on high speed, blend rose petals, vodka, grenadine and ice until rose petals and ice are finely chopped.

2. Strain through a fine sieve into a martini glass.

Makes 1 serving

Hot Pink Ginger

1 tbsp	freshly squeezed lime juice	15 mL
2 tsp	chopped ginger in syrup or pickled ginger	10 mL
1 tsp	grenadine	5 mL
2 oz	vodka	50 mL
2	ice cubes	2

1. In blender, on high speed, blend lime juice, ginger, grenadine, vodka and ice until smooth.

2. Pour into a martini glass.

Makes 1 serving

You can also garnish this translucent golden drink with a few blanched or raw almonds. For a more intense almond flavor, add 1 tbsp (15 mL) orgeat (almond) syrup.

Nutty Chocolate Bar

2	ice cubes	2
1 oz	vanilla vodka	25 mL
1 ½ oz	white crème de cacao	40 mL
½ oz	almond liqueur	15 mL
1	chocolate-covered almond	1

1. In blender, pulse ice until crushed. On high speed, blend in vodka, crème de cacao and almond liqueur until smooth.

2. Pour into a martini glass and garnish with chocolate-covered almond.

Chocolate Toffee

1 oz	vanilla vodka or vodka	25 mL
1 oz	toffee cream liqueur	25 mL
1 oz	white crème de cacao	25 mL
2	ice cubes	2
	Grated semisweet chocolate or 1 maraschino cherry	

1. In blender, on high speed, blend vodka, toffee liqueur, crème de cacao and ice until smooth.

2. Pour into a martini glass and sprinkle with chocolate or garnish with cherry.

Bitter Morning

Makes 1 serving

This is a nutritious, cleansing hangover drink. For a non-bitter drink, substitute peeled and seeded cucumber for the bitter melon.

This recipe contains a raw egg. If the food safety of raw eggs is a concern for you, use the pasteurized liquid whole egg instead.

1	egg (or ¼ cup/50 mL pasteurized liquid whole egg)	1
1 cup	chopped seeded bitter melon	250 mL
Pinch	salt	Pinch
Pinch	freshly ground black pepper	Pinch
Dash	Worcestershire sauce	Dash
Dash	hot pepper sauce	Dash
2 oz	vodka	50 mL
3	ice cubes	3

1. In blender, on high speed, blend egg, bitter melon, salt, pepper, Worcestershire sauce, hot pepper sauce, vodka and ice until smooth.

2. Pour into a highball glass.

Chipotle Bloody Mary

For a bit of protein to augment this spicy brunch drink, garnish with a skewer of cooked shrimp.

TIP

You can replace the canned chipotle peppers in adobo sauce with ½ tsp (2 mL) chipotle hot sauce.

⅔ cup	tomato juice	150 mL
2 tsp	freshly squeezed lime juice	10 mL
1 ½ tsp	minced canned chipotle pepper	7 mL
1 ½ oz	citrus vodka or vodka	40 mL
3	ice cubes	3
	Celery salt, for rimming	
1	celery stick	1
1	lime wedge	1

1. In blender, on high speed, blend tomato juice, lime juice, chipotle in adobo, vodka and ice until smooth.

2. Pour into a highball or old-fashioned glass rimmed with celery salt. Garnish with celery and lime.

Chili Pepper Bullshot

Rim your glass with salt, if you like, for this brunch (or hangover) drink. Try it also with a skewer of cherry tomatoes or of pickled onion and a folded slice of salami.

½ cup	chilled beef or vegetable stock	125 mL
¼ cup	tomato juice	50 mL
2 tsp	freshly squeezed lemon juice	10 mL
Dash	hot pepper sauce	Dash
Dash	Worcestershire sauce	Dash
2 oz	chili pepper vodka or vodka	50 mL
3	ice cubes	3
1	celery stick	1
1	lemon wedge	1

1. In blender, on high speed, blend stock, tomato juice, lemon juice, hot pepper sauce, Worcestershire sauce, vodka and ice until smooth.

2. Pour into a highball glass and garnish with celery stick and lemon wedge.

Frozen Caesar

A blender allows you to make a wonderfully refreshing frozen spin on a Caesar. For a variation on the taste, try using aquavit instead of vodka.

TIP

You can replace the tomato-clam juice with ⅓ cup (75 mL) tomato juice and 2 tbsp (25 mL) bottled clam juice.

½ cup	tomato-clam juice (see tip, at left)	125 mL
1 tsp	freshly squeezed lemon juice	5 mL
1 tsp	freshly squeezed lime juice	5 mL
Pinch	freshly ground black pepper	Pinch
Dash	Worcestershire sauce	Dash
2 oz	vodka or citrus vodka	25 mL
2	ice cubes	2
	Lime juice, for rimming	
	Celery salt, for rimming	
1	celery stick	1

1. In blender, on high speed, blend tomato-clam juice, lemon juice, lime juice, salt, pepper, Worcestershire sauce, vodka and ice until smooth.

2. Pour into an old-fashioned glass rimmed with lime juice and celery salt. Garnish with celery stick.

Barbecued Caesar

You can further garnish this unusual take on a Caesar — the brunch drink favored by Canadians — by replacing the celery with a skewered cooked shrimp, or skewer a cocktail onion, a folded slice of salami and a pimento-stuffed olive.

⅔ cup	tomato-clam juice or tomato juice	150 mL
1 tbsp	smoky barbecue sauce	15 mL
1½ oz	chili pepper vodka or vodka	40 mL
3	ice cubes	3
	Celery salt, for rimming	
1	celery stick	1
1	lime wedge	1

1. In blender, on high speed, blend tomato-clam juice, barbecue sauce, vodka and ice until smooth.

2. Pour into a highball or old-fashioned glass rimmed with celery salt. Garnish with celery and lime.

Makes 1 serving

Hair of the Clam

Although there are no true hangover remedies, this might make you feel better for a while — and you get a little nutrition at the same time.

1	peeled ripe or canned tomato	1
2 tbsp	clam juice	25 mL
2½ tsp	lemon juice, divided	12 mL
Pinch	salt	Pinch
Pinch	freshly ground black pepper	Pinch
Dash	hot pepper sauce	Dash
2 oz	vodka or aquavit	50 mL
1	ice cube	1
	Celery salt, for rimming	
1	short stalk celery	1

1. In blender, on high speed, blend tomato, clam juice, 2 tsp (10 mL) of the lemon juice, salt, pepper, hot pepper sauce, vodka and ice until smooth.

2. Wet the rim of an old-fashioned glass with the remaining lemon juice and dip in celery salt. Pour drink into glass and garnish with celery stalk.

Makes 1 serving

Vodka Alexander

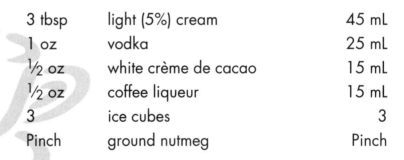

3 tbsp	light (5%) cream	45 mL
1 oz	vodka	25 mL
½ oz	white crème de cacao	15 mL
½ oz	coffee liqueur	15 mL
3	ice cubes	3
Pinch	ground nutmeg	Pinch

1. In blender, on high speed, blend cream, vodka, crème de cacao, coffee liqueur and ice until smooth.

2. Pour into a martini glass and sprinkle with nutmeg.

Makes 1 serving

Orgasmatron

This is a slushy version of the fave stagette shooter (don't try this one with no hands). For extra indulgence, top with a dollop of whipped cream and a maraschino cherry.

3 tbsp	light (5%) cream	45 mL
1/2 oz	vodka	15 mL
1/2 oz	Irish cream liqueur	15 mL
1/2 oz	coffee liqueur	15 mL
1/2 oz	almond liqueur	15 mL
2	ice cubes	2

1. In blender, on high speed, blend cream, vodka, Irish cream liqueur, coffee liqueur, almond liqueur and ice until smooth and frothy.

2. Pour into a martini glass.

Makes 1 serving

Apricot-Melonball

TIP

Look for apricot nectar or juice in bottles or cartons in the fruit juice section of well-stocked supermarkets and health food stores.

1/2 cup	apricot nectar or juice (see tip, at left)	125 mL
1/3 cup	cubed honeydew melon	75 mL
2 tbsp	light (5%) cream	25 mL
1 oz	vodka	25 mL
1 oz	melon liqueur	25 mL
2	ice cubes	2
1	skewer cubed honeydew melon	1

1. In blender, on high speed, blend apricot nectar, melon, cream, vodka, melon liqueur and ice until smooth.

2. Pour into a martini or wine glass and garnish with skewered melon.

Makes 1 serving

Chocolate Raspberry Parfait

2 tbsp	light (5%) cream	25 mL
¾ oz	raspberry vodka	22 mL
¾ oz	vanilla vodka	22 mL
¾ oz	white crème de cacao	22 mL
2	ice cubes	2
3	fresh raspberries	3

1. In blender, on high speed, blend cream, raspberry vodka, vanilla vodka, crème de cacao and ice until smooth.

2. Pour into a martini glass and garnish with raspberries.

Makes 1 serving

Chocolate-covered coffee beans make a great garnish for coffee-based cocktails. You can buy them at specialty coffee shops.

Creamy Toffee

¼ cup	light (5%) cream	50 mL
1 oz	toffee cream liqueur	25 mL
½ oz	vanilla vodka or vodka	15 mL
½ oz	coffee liqueur	15 mL
3	ice cubes	3
3	chocolate-covered coffee beans	3

1. In blender, on high speed, blend cream, toffee liqueur, vodka, coffee liqueur and ice until smooth.

2. Pour into an old-fashioned glass and garnish with coffee beans.

Berry Lassi

Makes 1 serving

Lassi is an Indian yogurt drink, here transformed into a delicious and indulgent cocktail.

4	frozen strawberries	4
1/3 cup	cranberry juice	75 mL
1/4 cup	plain or strawberry-flavored yogurt	50 mL
3 tbsp	frozen raspberries	45 mL
1 1/2 oz	vodka or raspberry vodka	40 mL
1	fresh strawberry (or 3 fresh raspberries)	1

1. In blender, on high speed, blend frozen strawberries, cranberry juice, yogurt, frozen raspberries and vodka until smooth.

2. Pour into a piña colada or old-fashioned glass and garnish with strawberry.

Makes 1 serving

Lemon-Papaya Lassi

3/4 cup	frozen cubed papaya	175 mL
1/2 cup	lemon sorbet	125 mL
1/4 cup	apricot nectar or juice (see tip, page 59)	50 mL
1/4 cup	plain or peach-flavored yogurt	50 mL
1 1/2 oz	citrus vodka or vodka	40 mL
1 tsp	papaya seeds (or 1 twist lemon rind or slice lemon)	5 mL

1. In blender, on high speed, blend papaya, sorbet, apricot nectar, yogurt and vodka until smooth.

2. Pour into a piña colada or highball glass and sprinkle with papaya seeds (or garnish with lemon).

Makes 1 serving

Mango Lassi

TIP

Look for mango nectar or juice or apricot nectar or juice in bottles or cartons in the fruit juice section of well-stocked supermarkets and health food stores.

¾ cup	frozen cubed mango	175 mL
½ cup	mango or lemon sorbet	125 mL
¼ cup	mango or apricot nectar or juice (see tip, at left)	50 mL
¼ cup	plain yogurt	50 mL
1½ oz	vodka	40 mL
1	skewer cubed fresh mango	1

1. In blender, on high speed, blend frozen mango, sorbet, mango nectar, yogurt and vodka until smooth.

2. Pour into a piña colada or highball glass and garnish with skewer of mango.

Makes 1 serving

Orange-Mango Lassi

¾ cup	frozen cubed mango	175 mL
½ cup	orange sorbet	125 mL
¼ cup	orange juice	50 mL
¼ cup	plain yogurt	50 mL
1½ oz	mandarin vodka or vodka	40 mL
1	slice orange	1

1. In blender, on high speed, blend mango, sorbet, orange juice, yogurt and vodka until smooth.

2. Pour into a piña colada or highball glass and garnish with orange slice.

Makes 1 serving # Pistachio Lassi

10	shelled pistachios	10
½ cup	vanilla frozen yogurt	125 mL
¼ cup	plain yogurt	50 mL
1 tbsp	Honey Syrup (see page 5)	15 mL
1 tsp	rosewater or orange blossom water (optional)	5 mL
Pinch	ground cardamom	Pinch
1½ oz	vanilla vodka or vodka	40 mL
1 tsp	crushed pistachios (or pinch ground cardamom)	5 mL

1. In blender, on high speed, blend pistachios, frozen yogurt, yogurt, Honey Syrup, rosewater (if using), cardamom and vodka until smooth.

2. Pour into a piña colada or old-fashioned glass and sprinkle with crushed pistachios.

Makes 1 serving # Chilled Latte

2 tbsp	light (5%) cream	25 mL
2 tbsp	chilled strong coffee or espresso	25 mL
1 oz	vodka	25 mL
1 oz	coffee liqueur	25 mL
3	ice cubes	3
3	chocolate-covered coffee beans (or grated semisweet chocolate)	3

1. In blender, on high speed, blend cream, coffee, vodka, coffee liqueur and ice until smooth.

2. Pour into a large martini or old-fashioned glass and garnish with coffee beans (or sprinkle with chocolate).

Shooter Nog

Makes about
2½ cups (625 mL)

This recipe contains raw egg yolks. If the food safety of raw eggs is a concern for you, use the pasteurized liquid whole egg instead. The 'nog will not thicken as much, but you can add some vanilla ice cream to give a thicker consistency, if desired.

6	egg yolks (or ⅔ cup/150 mL pasteurized liquid whole egg)	6
½ cup	granulated sugar	125 mL
1½ tsp	vanilla	7 mL
½ tsp	ground nutmeg	2 mL
13 oz	vodka (about ½ bottle)	375 mL
3 oz	cognac or other brandy	75 mL
1½ oz	Scotch whisky	40 mL

1. In blender, on high speed, blend egg yolks and sugar until creamy. Blend in vanilla, nutmeg, vodka, cognac and Scotch until smooth.

2. Pour into a freezer-proof bottle or container and store in the freezer for up to 1 month. Serve in shot glasses.

Morning Glory Fizz

Makes 1 serving

This recipe contains a raw egg white. If the food safety of raw eggs is a concern for you, use the pasteurized liquid egg white instead.

1	egg white (or 2 tbsp/25 mL pasteurized liquid egg white)	1
2 tbsp	freshly squeezed lime juice	25 mL
1½ tsp	confectioner's (icing) sugar	7 mL
2 oz	vodka	50 mL
½ oz	anise liqueur, such as Pernod	15 mL
2	ice cubes	2
2 tbsp	soda water or seltzer (approx.)	25 mL

1. In blender, on high speed, blend egg white, lime juice, sugar, vodka, anise liqueur and ice until smooth.

2. Pour into a highball glass and top with soda.

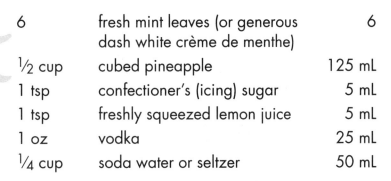

Minty Pineapple Spritz

Makes 1 serving

6	fresh mint leaves (or generous dash white crème de menthe)	6
1/2 cup	cubed pineapple	125 mL
1 tsp	confectioner's (icing) sugar	5 mL
1 tsp	freshly squeezed lemon juice	5 mL
1 oz	vodka	25 mL
1/4 cup	soda water or seltzer	50 mL

1. In blender, on high speed, blend mint, pineapple, sugar, lemon juice and vodka until smooth.

2. Pour into a large highball glass filled with ice and top with soda.

Rosy Pom Refresher

Makes 1 serving

TIP

Pomegranate cocktails can be made with purchased pomegranate juice or with freshly squeezed juice. To juice a pomegranate, cut it in half and use a citrus reamer or juicer; strain. One large pomegranate will yield about 1/2 cup (125 mL) juice.

1/4 cup	pomegranate juice (see tip, at left)	50 mL
1 1/2 oz	currant vodka or vodka	40 mL
2	ice cubes	2
1/2 cup	chilled lemon-lime soda	125 mL

1. In blender, on high speed, blend pomegranate juice, vodka and ice until smooth.

2. Pour into an old-fashioned or wine glass and top with lemon-lime soda.

The Fizzmopolitan

Author Alison Kent's husband, Drazen, invented this drink when he thought she was "taking too long" between bouts of experimental cocktail concoctions. It was a hit.

2	ice cubes	2
1/4 cup	chilled soda water	50 mL
2 tbsp	pomegranate juice (see tip, page 52)	25 mL
1 tbsp	Simple Syrup (see page 5)	15 mL
2 tsp	freshly squeezed lime juice	10 mL
1 tsp	freshly squeezed lemon juice	5 mL
1 1/2 oz	vodka	40 mL
1/2 oz	orange liqueur	15 mL
1 tsp	pomegranate seeds (or 1 twist of orange rind)	5 mL

1. In blender, pulse ice until crushed. On high speed, blend in soda water, pomegranate juice, Simple Syrup, lime juice, lemon juice, vodka and orange liqueur until smooth and frothy.

2. Pour into a large martini or wine glass and garnish with pomegranate seeds (or orange twist).

Island Refresher

1/3 cup	cranberry-raspberry juice	75 mL
1 oz	raspberry vodka or vodka	25 mL
1/2 oz	white rum	15 mL
3	ice cubes	3
1	slice orange or pineapple wedge	1

1. In blender, on high speed, blend cranberry-raspberry juice, vodka, rum and ice until smooth.

2. Pour into an old-fashioned glass and garnish with orange or pineapple.

Grapefruit Cooler

¼ cup	pink grapefruit juice	50 mL
2 tbsp	cranberry juice	25 mL
1 oz	cranberry vodka or vodka	25 mL
½ oz	orange liqueur	15 mL
3	ice cubes	3
3	frozen cranberries (or 1 twist orange rind)	3

1. In blender, on high speed, blend grapefruit juice, cranberry juice, vodka, orange liqueur and ice until smooth.

2. Pour into a large martini or wine glass and garnish with cranberries (or orange twist).

Citrus Iced Tea

Variation

Instead of tea, you can use a herbal tisane, such as lemon or orange zinger, for this cocktail.

3	ice cubes	3
1 cup	chilled strong orange pekoe tea	250 mL
2 tbsp	freshly squeezed orange juice	25 mL
1 tbsp	freshly squeezed lime juice	15 mL
1 tbsp	Simple Syrup (see page 5)	15 mL
1 tsp	chopped crystallized ginger	5 mL
2 oz	citrus vodka or vodka	50 mL
1	twist orange, lime or lemon rind	1

1. In blender, pulse ice until crushed. On high speed, blend in tea, orange juice, lime juice, Simple Syrup, ginger and vodka until slushy.

2. Pour into an old-fashioned glass and garnish with citrus twist.

Iced Green Tea

Makes 1 serving

Variation

For a change of flavor, you can make this drink with orange pekoe or lemon zinger tea.

3	ice cubes	3
1 cup	chilled strong green tea	250 mL
2 tbsp	freshly squeezed lemon juice	25 mL
1 tbsp	Simple Syrup (see page 5)	15 mL
1 tbsp	chopped fresh mint	15 mL
2 oz	citrus vodka or vodka	50 mL
1	sprig fresh mint	1

1. In blender, pulse ice until crushed. On high speed, blend in green tea, lemon juice, Simple Syrup, chopped mint and vodka until slushy.

2. Pour into an old-fashioned glass and garnish with mint sprig.

Rasp-Orange Iced Tea

Makes 1 serving

This cocktail will prove to be a killer refreshment on a hot summer day.

1/4 cup	chilled strong orange pekoe tea	50 mL
2 tbsp	frozen raspberry juice concentrate	25 mL
2 tbsp	frozen orange juice concentrate	25 mL
1 tbsp	freshly squeezed lemon juice	15 mL
1 tbsp	Simple Syrup (see page 5)	15 mL
1 1/2 oz	orange vodka or vodka	40 mL
3	ice cubes	3
1	slice orange	1
3	fresh raspberries	3

1. In blender, on high speed, blend tea, raspberry juice concentrate, orange juice concentrate, lemon juice, Simple Syrup, vodka and ice until slushy.

2. Pour into a highball glass and garnish with orange slice and raspberries.

Makes 1 serving

Watermelon Lemonade

This frothy pink summer drink can be garnished with a sprinkle of chopped crystallized ginger, a triangle of watermelon or a twist of lemon rind. For a lighter texture, strain through a fine sieve.

¾ cup	frozen cubed seedless watermelon	175 mL
3 tbsp	cranberry juice	45 mL
2 tbsp	freshly squeezed lemon juice	25 mL
1 tbsp	Simple Syrup (see page 5)	15 mL
1 tsp	chopped crystallized ginger	5 mL
1 ½ oz	watermelon vodka or citrus vodka	40 mL
½ oz	melon liqueur	15 mL

1. In blender, on high speed, blend watermelon, cranberry juice, lemon juice, Simple Syrup, ginger, vodka and melon liqueur until smooth.

2. Pour into a piña colada or old-fashioned glass.

Makes 1 serving

Pineapple Lemonade

¼ cup	frozen lemonade concentrate	50 mL
¼ cup	pineapple juice	50 mL
1 ½ oz	vodka	40 mL
2	ice cubes	2
1	pineapple wedge or slice lemon	1

1. In blender, on high speed, blend lemonade concentrate, pineapple juice, vodka and ice until smooth.

2. Pour into a piña colada or old-fashioned glass and garnish with pineapple wedge or lemon slice.

Sparkling Black Currant Lemonade

Makes 1 serving

2 tbsp	frozen lemonade concentrate	25 mL
2 oz	vodka	50 mL
1 oz	crème de cassis	25 mL
6	ice cubes	6
¼ cup	soda water or seltzer	50 mL
1	slice lemon	1

1. In blender, on high speed, blend lemonade concentrate, vodka, crème de cassis and ice until smooth.

2. Pour into a highball glass and top with soda. Garnish with lemon slice.

Frosty Screwdriver

Makes 1 serving

¼ cup	frozen orange juice concentrate	50 mL
2 oz	vodka	50 mL
½ oz	orange liqueur	15 mL
6	ice cubes	6
1	slice orange	1

1. In blender, on high speed, blend orange juice concentrate, vodka, orange liqueur and ice until smooth.

2. Pour into a highball glass and garnish with orange slice.

Makes 1 serving

Winter Whippet

This is a seasonal version of the Florida gin and grapefruit juice cocktail known as a Greyhound.

¼ cup	frozen grapefruit juice concentrate	50 mL
2 oz	vodka	50 mL
6	ice cubes	6

1. In blender, on high speed, blend grapefruit juice concentrate, vodka and ice until slushy.

2. Pour into a highball glass.

Makes 1 serving

Pink Whippet

¼ cup	frozen pink grapefruit juice concentrate	50 mL
1 tsp	grenadine	5 mL
2 oz	vodka	50 mL
2 dashes	angostura bitters	2 dashes
6	ice cubes	6

1. In blender, on high speed, blend grapefruit juice concentrate, grenadine, vodka, bitters and ice until slushy.

2. Pour into an old-fashioned glass.

Makes 1 serving

Moscow Mule Slushy

The Moscow Mule was created when Russian vodka began to be imported to North America.

1/3 cup	lime sorbet	75 mL
2 oz	vodka	50 mL
1/4 cup	chilled ginger beer	50 mL
1	slice lime	1

TIP

You can replace the ginger beer with ginger ale and sprinkle with 1 tsp (5 mL) chopped crystallized ginger.

1. In blender, on high speed, blend lime sorbet and vodka until slushy.

2. Pour into an old-fashioned glass and top with ginger beer. Garnish with lime.

Makes 1 serving

Smooth 'n' Orange

1/4 cup	orange sorbet	50 mL
1/4 cup	orange juice	50 mL
1 1/2 oz	orange liqueur	40 mL
1/2 oz	vodka	15 mL
2	ice cubes	2
1	twist orange rind	1

1. In blender, on high speed, blend sorbet, orange juice, orange liqueur, vodka and ice until smooth.

2. Pour into a martini glass and garnish with orange twist.

Makes 1 serving

Cran-Raspberry Smoothie

¼ cup	raspberry sorbet	50 mL
3 tbsp	cranberry juice	45 mL
1 oz	cranberry or raspberry vodka	25 mL
1 oz	raspberry liqueur or framboise	25 mL
3	frozen cranberries or fresh raspberries	3

1. In blender, on high speed, blend sorbet, cranberry juice, vodka and raspberry liqueur until smooth.

2. Pour into a large martini or wine glass and garnish with cranberries or raspberries.

Makes 1 serving

Rosemary-Grapefruit Cooler

1 cup	lemon sorbet	250 mL
½ cup	pink grapefruit juice	125 mL
¼ tsp	chopped fresh rosemary	1 mL
Pinch	freshly ground black pepper	Pinch
2 oz	citrus vodka or vodka	50 mL
1	sprig fresh rosemary	1
	Additional freshly ground black pepper (optional)	

1. In blender, on high speed, blend sorbet, grapefruit juice, rosemary, pepper and vodka until slushy.

2. Strain through a fine sieve into an old-fashioned glass and garnish with rosemary sprig. Sprinkle with pepper, if desired.

Tomato-Basil Refresher

You can replace or augment the lemon garnish with a cherry tomato, skewered along with a fresh basil leaf.

1 cup	tomato juice	250 mL
¼ cup	lemon sorbet	50 mL
4 tsp	chopped fresh basil	20 mL
1½ oz	citrus vodka or vodka	40 mL
1	slice lemon	1

1. In blender, on high speed, blend tomato juice, sorbet, basil and vodka until smooth.

2. Strain through a fine sieve into an old-fashioned glass and garnish with lemon.

Ambrosia Freeze

You can garnish this vegetable and fruit medley with a pineapple wedge, a slice of orange or a carrot stick.

⅓ cup	carrot juice	75 mL
¼ cup	orange sorbet	50 mL
2 tbsp	frozen pineapple juice concentrate	25 mL
1½ oz	citrus vodka or vodka	40 mL

1. In blender, on high speed, blend carrot juice, sorbet, pineapple juice concentrate and vodka until smooth.

2. Pour into a piña colada glass.

Makes 1 serving

Creamy Citrus Ice

⅓ cup	lemon sorbet	75 mL
¼ cup	vanilla ice cream	50 mL
2 oz	citrus or vanilla vodka	50 mL
1 oz	orange liqueur	25 mL
1	twist orange or lemon rind	1

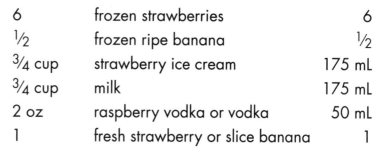

1. In blender, on high speed, blend sorbet, ice cream, vodka and orange liqueur until smooth.

2. Pour into a piña colada or old-fashioned glass and garnish with orange twist.

Makes 1 serving

Berry Cow

6	frozen strawberries	6
½	frozen ripe banana	½
¾ cup	strawberry ice cream	175 mL
¾ cup	milk	175 mL
2 oz	raspberry vodka or vodka	50 mL
1	fresh strawberry or slice banana	1

1. In blender, on high speed, blend frozen strawberries, frozen banana, ice cream, milk and vodka until smooth.

2. Pour into a piña colada or old-fashioned glass and garnish with strawberry or banana slice.

Creamy Cherry Fizz

This intensely purple, frothy milkshake-like drink makes for an adult-style old-fashioned malt shop experience.

2	ice cubes	2
2 tbsp	chilled black cherry soda	25 mL
2 tbsp	vanilla ice cream	25 mL
1 oz	vanilla vodka	25 mL
1 oz	cherry brandy	25 mL
1	fresh cherry or maraschino cherry	1

1. In blender, pulse ice until crushed. On high speed, blend in black cherry soda, ice cream, vodka and brandy until smooth.

2. Pour into a martini glass and garnish with cherry.

Leaping Leprechauns

Of course you need a new St. Patrick's Day drink.

¼ cup	vanilla ice cream	50 mL
1½ oz	vanilla vodka or vodka	40 mL
½ oz	white crème de cacao	15 mL
½ oz	green crème de menthe	15 mL
1	green maraschino cherry	1

1. In blender, on high speed, blend ice cream, vodka, crème de cacao and crème de menthe until smooth.

2. Pour into a martini glass and garnish with cherry.

Makes 1 serving

Mint-Chocolate Shake

2	chocolate-covered peppermint sticks or patties	2
¾ cup	chocolate mint or chocolate ice cream	175 mL
½ cup	milk	125 mL
1 tbsp	chopped fresh mint	15 mL
2 oz	vanilla vodka or vodka	50 mL
1	sprig fresh mint	1
1 tsp	grated semisweet chocolate	5 mL

1. In blender, on high speed, blend peppermint sticks, ice cream, milk, chopped mint and vodka until smooth.

2. Pour into a martini or wine glass, garnish with mint sprig and sprinkle with chocolate.

Makes 1 serving

This cocktail will bring you back to your childhood. For an even deeper voyage back to your youth, sprinkle it with crushed malted chocolate candies.

Chocolate Malted

1 cup	chocolate ice cream	250 mL
¾ cup	milk	175 mL
2 tbsp	malted milk powder, such as Ovaltine	25 mL
1½ oz	vanilla vodka or vodka	40 mL
½ oz	crème de cacao	15 mL

1. In blender, on high speed, blend ice cream, milk, malted milk powder, vodka and crème de cacao until smooth.

2. Pour into a highball glass.

Makes 1 serving

Choco-Orange Smoothie

¼ cup	chocolate ice cream	50 mL
¼ cup	orange sorbet	50 mL
1 tsp	finely grated orange zest	5 mL
1½ oz	mandarin vodka or vodka	40 mL
1 oz	white crème de cacao	25 mL
1	twist orange rind	1
Pinch	grated semisweet chocolate	Pinch

1. In blender, on high speed, blend ice cream, sorbet, orange zest, vodka and crème de cacao until smooth.

2. Pour into a piña colada or wine glass, garnish with orange twist and sprinkle with chocolate.

Makes 1 serving

Nutty Symphony

Why not finish a festive meal with a "Nutty Symphony"?

¼ cup	vanilla or coffee ice cream	50 mL
1 oz	vanilla vodka or vodka	25 mL
¾ oz	hazelnut liqueur	22 mL
½ oz	Irish cream liqueur	15 mL
½ oz	crème de cacao	15 mL
Pinch	ground nutmeg	Pinch

1. In blender, on high speed, blend ice cream, vodka, hazelnut liqueur, Irish cream liqueur and crème de cacao until smooth.

2. Pour into a piña colada or old-fashioned glass and sprinkle with nutmeg.

Peanut Butter and Jam

Garnish this escape to childhood with a slice of banana, a maraschino cherry or a fresh strawberry.

TIP

Look for almond milk in the milk or health food section of grocery stores, near the soy milk.

½	frozen ripe banana	½
½ cup	strawberry ice cream	125 mL
½ cup	almond milk (see tip, at left) or light (5%) cream	125 mL
2 tbsp	smooth natural peanut butter	25 mL
2 oz	raspberry vodka or vodka	50 mL
½ oz	raspberry liqueur or framboise	15 mL
½ oz	crème de banane	15 mL

1. In blender, on high speed, blend banana, ice cream, almond milk, peanut butter, vodka, raspberry liqueur and crème de banane until smooth.

2. Pour into a highball glass.

Paralyzer

For extra decadence, you can replace the chocolate-covered coffee beans with ½ chocolate-covered hazelnut (such as Ferrero Rocher).

¼ cup	coffee ice cream	50 mL
1 oz	vanilla vodka or vodka	25 mL
½ oz	Irish cream liqueur	15 mL
½ oz	coffee liqueur	15 mL
½ oz	hazelnut liqueur	15 mL
3	chocolate-covered coffee beans	3

1. In blender, on high speed, blend ice cream, vodka, Irish cream liqueur, coffee liqueur and hazelnut liqueur until smooth.

2. Pour into a piña colada or old-fashioned glass and garnish with coffee beans.

White Russian Shake

Makes 1 serving

For a lower-alcohol version, reduce the vodka and increase the milk by equal amounts.

⅓ cup	vanilla ice cream	75 mL
2 tbsp	milk	25 mL
3 oz	vodka	75 mL
1 oz	coffee liqueur	15 mL

1. In blender, on high speed, blend ice cream, milk, vodka and coffee liqueur until smooth.

2. Pour into an old-fashioned glass.

Brown Russian Shake

Makes 1 serving

For a lower-alcohol version, reduce the vodka and increase the milk by equal amounts.

¼ cup	chocolate ice cream	50 mL
2 tbsp	milk	25 mL
3 oz	vodka	75 mL
1½ oz	coffee liqueur	40 mL
2	ice cubes	2
2 tsp	grated bittersweet chocolate	10 mL

1. In blender, on high speed, blend ice cream, milk, vodka, coffee liqueur and ice until smooth.

2. Pour into an old-fashioned glass and sprinkle with chocolate.

Makes 1 serving

Chocolate Black Russian

½ cup	chocolate ice cream	125 mL
1 ½ oz	vodka or vanilla vodka	40 mL
¾ oz	coffee liqueur	22 mL
1	maraschino cherry (optional)	1

1. In blender, on high speed, blend ice cream, vodka and coffee liqueur until smooth.

2. Pour into a large martini glass and garnish with cherry, if desired.

Makes 1 serving

Candy cane lovers will love this festive drink.

Creamy Candy Cane

¼ cup	vanilla ice cream	50 mL
1 oz	vanilla vodka	25 mL
½ oz	white crème de menthe	15 mL
½ oz	white crème de cacao	15 mL
1	small mint-flavored candy cane	1

1. In blender, on high speed, blend ice cream, vodka, crème de menthe and crème de cacao until smooth.

2. Pour into a piña colada or old-fashioned glass and garnish with candy cane.

rum

RUM IS THE DRINK of the Americas. It originated in Puerto Rico, or perhaps Barbados, during the 17th century. Rum is a by-product of the sugar business, in that most rums are distilled from molasses, which is a residue of sugar refining (occasionally, rum is produced directly from cane juice). Wherever sugar is grown, rum is produced. Because of its subtropical and tropical origins, rum has always been paired with tropical fruits in blended drinks, and the results proclaim this liquor's propensity to augment and enhance fruit flavors.

White, or light, rum, which is distilled in stainless steel tanks and doesn't need aging, has only a hint of cane flavor and is the lightest blending liquor after vodka. It tends to have a hotter mouth-feel than vodka, but this is usually masked when it is blended into a cocktail. We prefer aged amber (also called gold or medium) rum for most drinks, as it imparts a subtle flavor of molasses, with woody and vanilla overtones. Dark rum will often shine through the fruit flavors it may be blended with in a cocktail; whether you want that or not is a personal choice. Fine añejo (aged) rums are great for sipping straight up or on the rocks, but their more subtle characteristics will be lost in blended drinks — stick to good average-priced brands for blender cocktails.

Spiced rum (such as Captain Morgan) is a popular ingredient in cocktails, as is coconut rum (such as Malibu). There are many other types of flavored rums, but we most often prefer to add the flavors ourselves with fresh ingredients. However, you can generally substitute citrus-flavored and other flavored white rums for similarly flavored vodkas. If we don't specify what kind of rum to use, follow your personal preferences.

RUM RECIPES

continued next page…

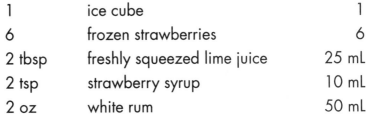

Makes 1 serving

This is the blender version of the classic cocktail.

Frozen Daiquiri

2	ice cubes	2
2 tbsp	freshly squeezed lime juice	25 mL
1 tsp	confectioner's (icing) sugar	5 mL
2 oz	white rum	50 mL

1. In blender, pulse ice until crushed. On high speed, blend in lime juice, sugar and rum until slushy.

2. Pour into an old-fashioned or martini glass.

Makes 1 serving

Frozen Strawberry Daiquiri

1	ice cube	1
6	frozen strawberries	6
2 tbsp	freshly squeezed lime juice	25 mL
2 tsp	strawberry syrup	10 mL
2 oz	white rum	50 mL

1. In blender, pulse ice and strawberries until ice is crushed. On high speed, blend in lime juice, strawberry syrup and rum until slushy.

2. Pour into an old-fashioned or martini glass.

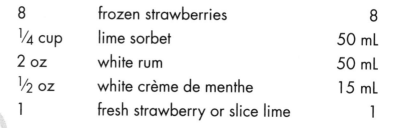

Makes 1 serving

Strawberry Mint Daiquiri

8	frozen strawberries	8
¼ cup	lime sorbet	50 mL
2 oz	white rum	50 mL
½ oz	white crème de menthe	15 mL
1	fresh strawberry or slice lime	1

1. In blender, on high speed, blend frozen strawberries, sorbet, rum and crème de menthe until slushy.

2. Pour into an old-fashioned glass and garnish with strawberry or lime slice.

Makes 1 serving

Frozen Banana Daiquiri

3	ice cubes	3
½	banana	½
2 tbsp	freshly squeezed lime juice	25 mL
2 oz	white rum	50 mL
1 oz	crème de banane	25 mL

1. In blender, pulse ice and banana until ice is crushed. On high speed, blend in lime juice, rum and crème de banane until slushy.

2. Pour into an old-fashioned or martini glass.

Frozen Blue-Banana Daiquiri

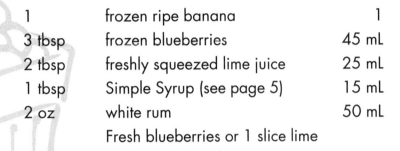

1	frozen ripe banana	1
3 tbsp	frozen blueberries	45 mL
2 tbsp	freshly squeezed lime juice	25 mL
1 tbsp	Simple Syrup (see page 5)	15 mL
2 oz	white rum	50 mL
	Fresh blueberries or 1 slice lime	

1. In blender, on high speed, blend banana, frozen blueberries, lime juice, Simple Syrup and rum until slushy.

2. Pour into an old-fashioned glass and garnish with blueberries or lime slice.

Frozen Peach Daiquiri

TIP

To peel a fresh peach, submerge it in boiling water for 10 to 15 seconds to loosen the skin. Or use drained canned peaches or frozen sliced peaches.

2	ice cubes	2
1/2 cup	cubed peeled peaches (see tip, at left)	125 mL
2 tbsp	freshly squeezed lime juice	25 mL
1 1/2 tsp	confectioner's (icing) sugar	7 mL
2 oz	white rum	50 mL
1 oz	peach schnapps	25 mL

1. In blender, pulse ice and peach until ice is crushed. On high speed, blend in lime juice, sugar, rum and peach schnapps until slushy.

2. Pour into an old-fashioned or martini glass.

Makes 1 serving

Hemingway Daiquiri

The original drink from which this is adapted was created for the American author in Cuba in 1921.

¼ cup	grapefruit juice	50 mL
4 tsp	freshly squeezed lime juice	20 mL
4 tsp	Simple Syrup (see page 5)	20 mL
2 tsp	grenadine	10 mL
2 oz	white rum	50 mL
3	ice cubes	3
1	lime wedge	1
1	maraschino cherry (optional)	1

1. In blender, on high speed, blend grapefruit juice, lime juice, Simple Syrup, grenadine, rum and ice until slushy.

2. Pour into a piña colada or old-fashioned glass and garnish with lime wedge and cherry, if desired.

Makes 1 serving

Frozen Lichee Daiquiri

2	ice cubes	2
5	canned lichees, drained	5
2 tbsp	freshly squeezed lime juice	25 mL
2 tsp	syrup from canned lichees	10 mL
2 oz	white rum	50 mL

1. In blender, pulse ice and lichees until ice is crushed. On high speed, blend in lime juice, syrup and rum until slushy.

2. Pour into an old-fashioned or martini glass.

Makes 1 serving

Frozen Coconut Daiquiri

2	ice cubes	2
2 tbsp	freshly squeezed lime juice	25 mL
2 tsp	creamed coconut	10 mL
1 ½ oz	white rum	40 mL
1 oz	coconut rum	25 mL

1. In blender, pulse ice until crushed. On high speed, blend in lime juice, creamed coconut, and white and coconut rums until slushy.

2. Pour into an old-fashioned or martini glass.

Makes 1 serving

Piña Colada

Creamed coconut is already sweetened. You can substitute coconut milk; use ¼ cup (50 mL) from the top of the can (the coconut cream) and add 1 tbsp (15 mL) Simple Syrup (see page 5).

1 cup	cubed pineapple	250 mL
2 tbsp	creamed coconut	25 mL
1 ½ oz	amber or white rum	40 mL
3	ice cubes	3
1	lime wedge (optional)	1

1. In blender, on high speed, blend pineapple, creamed coconut, rum and ice until smooth.

2. Pour into a highball glass and garnish with lime wedge, if desired.

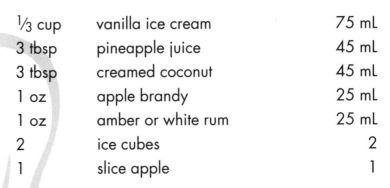

Makes 1 serving

Apple Colada

⅓ cup	vanilla ice cream	75 mL
3 tbsp	pineapple juice	45 mL
3 tbsp	creamed coconut	45 mL
1 oz	apple brandy	25 mL
1 oz	amber or white rum	25 mL
2	ice cubes	2
1	slice apple	1

1. In blender, on high speed, blend ice cream, pineapple juice, creamed coconut, apple brandy, rum and ice until smooth.

2. Pour into a piña colada glass and garnish with apple slice.

Makes 1 serving

Strawberry Colada

You can turn this into a raspberry colada by substituting ¾ cup (175 mL) fresh or frozen raspberries for the strawberries.

12	fresh or frozen strawberries	12
2 tbsp	creamed coconut	25 mL
2 tbsp	vanilla ice cream	25 mL
2 oz	amber or white rum	50 mL
3	ice cubes	3
1	lemon or lime wedge (optional)	1

1. In blender, on high speed, blend strawberries, creamed coconut, ice cream, rum and ice until smooth.

2. Pour into a highball glass and garnish with lemon wedge, if desired.

Makes 1 serving

Trinidad Piña Colada

1 cup	cubed pineapple	250 mL
2 tbsp	creamed coconut	25 mL
Pinch	salt	Pinch
1 1/2 oz	amber or white rum	40 mL
4 dashes	angostura bitters	4 dashes
3	ice cubes	3

1. In blender, on high speed, blend pineapple, creamed coconut, salt, rum, bitters and ice until smooth.

2. Pour into a highball glass.

Makes 1 serving

Aqua Piña Colada

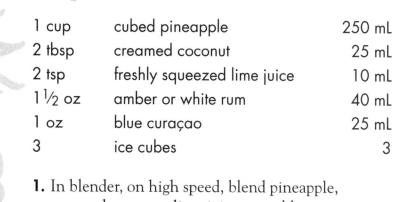

1 cup	cubed pineapple	250 mL
2 tbsp	creamed coconut	25 mL
2 tsp	freshly squeezed lime juice	10 mL
1 1/2 oz	amber or white rum	40 mL
1 oz	blue curaçao	25 mL
3	ice cubes	3

1. In blender, on high speed, blend pineapple, creamed coconut, lime juice, rum, blue curaçao and ice until smooth.

2. Pour into a highball glass.

Almond Colada

¼ cup	pineapple juice	50 mL
3 tbsp	creamed coconut	45 mL
1 oz	almond liqueur	25 mL
1 oz	amber or white rum	25 mL
3	ice cubes	3
1	pineapple wedge	1
1	maraschino cherry	1

1. In blender, on high speed, blend pineapple juice, creamed coconut, almond liqueur, rum and ice until smooth.

2. Pour into a piña colada glass and garnish with pineapple wedge and cherry.

Piña Colada Martini

⅓ cup	cubed pineapple	75 mL
1 tsp	freshly squeezed lime juice	5 mL
2 oz	coconut rum	50 mL
1	ice cube	1

1. In blender, on high speed, blend pineapple, lime juice, coconut rum and ice until smooth.

2. Pour into a martini glass.

Pilipino Piña

½ cup	cubed pineapple	125 mL
2 tsp	cane syrup or Simple Syrup (see page 5)	10 mL
2 tsp	freshly squeezed lime juice	10 mL
2 oz	amber rum	50 mL
4	ice cubes	4

1. In blender, on high speed, blend pineapple, syrup, lime juice, rum and ice until smooth.

2. Pour into a highball glass.

Tomahawk

2 tbsp	frozen cranberry cocktail concentrate	25 mL
2 tbsp	frozen pineapple juice concentrate	25 mL
2 oz	white or amber rum	50 mL
½ oz	orange liqueur	15 mL
6	ice cubes	6
1	lime wedge	1

1. In blender, on high speed, blend cranberry cocktail and pineapple juice concentrates, rum, orange liqueur and ice until smooth.

2. Pour into an old-fashioned glass and garnish with lime wedge.

Mary Pickford

This cocktail is adapted from one created in Cuba during Prohibition for the film star Mary Pickford.

¼ cup	frozen pineapple juice concentrate	50 mL
1 tsp	grenadine	5 mL
1½ oz	white rum	40 mL
½ oz	cherry brandy	15 mL
2	ice cubes	2
1	pineapple wedge	1
1	maraschino cherry	1

1. In blender, on high speed, blend pineapple juice concentrate, grenadine, rum, brandy and ice until smooth.

2. Pour into an old-fashioned or cocktail glass and garnish with pineapple wedge and cherry.

The Wave

Garnish this drink inspired by the Caribbean spice island of Grenadine with a pineapple wedge studded with whole cloves.

½ cup	pineapple juice	125 mL
1 tsp	grenadine	5 mL
1 oz	spiced rum	25 mL
1 oz	peach schnapps	25 mL
3	ice cubes	3

1. In blender, on high speed, blend pineapple juice, grenadine, rum, peach schnapps and ice until smooth.

2. Pour into an old-fashioned glass.

Makes 1 serving

Coconut Rum Punch

½ cup	coconut milk	125 mL
2 tsp	palm sugar or light brown sugar	10 mL
1 tsp	freshly squeezed lime juice	5 mL
2 oz	amber rum	50 mL
2	ice cubes	2

1. In blender, on high speed, blend coconut milk, sugar, lime juice, rum and ice cubes until smooth.

2. Pour into a large stemmed punch glass or coconut shell.

Makes 1 serving

Mock Multo-Buko

For a real multo-buko, replace the coconut milk with 1 cup (250 mL) fresh young coconut (buko in Tagalog), including its gelatinous flesh.

½ cup	coconut milk	125 mL
1 tbsp	freshly squeezed lime juice	15 mL
1 tbsp	Simple Syrup (see page 5)	15 mL
2 oz	amber rum	50 mL
6	ice cubes	6
1	slice lime	1

1. In blender, on high speed, blend coconut milk, lime juice, Simple Syrup, rum and ice until smooth.

2. Pour into a large highball glass or coconut shell and garnish with lime slice.

Monkey Business

Makes 1 serving

Creamed coconut is already sweetened. You can substitute coconut milk; use 1/4 cup (50 mL) from the top of the can (the coconut cream) and add 1 tbsp (15 mL) Simple Syrup (see page 5).

1/2 cup	cubed fresh pineapple or drained unsweetened canned pineapple chunks	125 mL
2 tbsp	creamed coconut	25 mL
1 1/2 oz	dark rum	40 mL
1 1/2 oz	amber or white rum	40 mL
1/2 oz	crème de banane	15 mL
2	ice cubes	2
1	lime wedge	1

1. In blender, on high speed, blend pineapple, creamed coconut, dark and amber rums, crème de banane and ice until smooth.

2. Pour into a highball glass and garnish with lime wedge.

Bananarama

Makes 1 serving

1/2	banana	1/2
2 tbsp	freshly squeezed lime juice	25 mL
1 1/2 tsp	confectioner's (icing) sugar	7 mL
2 oz	white, amber or dark rum	50 mL
3	ice cubes	3

1. In blender, on high speed, blend banana, lime juice, sugar, rum and ice until smooth.

2. Pour into a highball glass.

From bottom left, clockwise: Frozen Cosmo (page 39), Mango Sparkler (page 180), Lemongrass Martini (page 38), Sapphire Fizz (page 202), and Frozen Margarita (page 164)

Overleaf: Frozen Banana Daiquiri (page 86)

Cocobananaberry

Makes 1 serving

¼ cup	pineapple juice	50 mL
2 tbsp	creamed coconut	25 mL
1 tbsp	freshly squeezed lime juice	15 mL
1 oz	white or amber rum	25 mL
½ oz	crème de cassis	15 mL
½ oz	crème de banane	15 mL
3	ice cubes	3
1	slice lime	1

1. In blender, on high speed, blend pineapple juice, creamed coconut, lime juice, rum, crème de cassis, crème de banane and ice until smooth.

2. Pour into a piña colada glass and garnish with lime slice.

Bee's Bananarama

Makes 1 serving

½	banana	½
1 tbsp	liquid honey	15 mL
2 tsp	freshly squeezed lemon juice	10 mL
1 oz	white or amber rum	25 mL
1 oz	brandy	25 mL
3	ice cubes	3
Pinch	ground cinnamon	Pinch

1. In blender, on high speed, blend banana, honey, lemon juice, rum, brandy and ice until smooth.

2. Pour into a highball glass and sprinkle with cinnamon.

Overleaf: Tropical Spiced Tea (page 109)

Gin Mint Julep (page 133)

Tiger Stripes

2 tbsp	chocolate syrup	25 mL
½	banana	½
1 cup	milk	250 mL
1 ½ oz	amber rum	40 mL
5	ice cubes	5

1. Drizzle chocolate syrup into a chilled highball glass, rotating glass as you drizzle to form a spiral.

2. In blender, on high speed, blend banana, milk, rum and ice until smooth. Pour into glass.

Florida Keys Rum Runner

2 tbsp	frozen fruit punch concentrate	25 mL
2 tsp	grenadine	10 mL
1 tsp	freshly squeezed lime juice	5 mL
1 oz	dark rum	25 mL
½ oz	crème de cassis or blackberry liqueur	15 mL
½ oz	crème de banane	15 mL
4	ice cubes	4

1. In blender, on high speed, blend fruit punch concentrate, grenadine, lime juice, rum, crème de cassis, crème de banane and ice until smooth.

2. Pour into a highball or large stemmed punch glass.

Makes 1 serving

White Berry

6	frozen strawberries	6
1/3 cup	white cranberry juice	75 mL
1 tsp	freshly squeezed lemon juice	5 mL
1 1/2 oz	white rum	40 mL
1	fresh strawberry (or 3 frozen cranberries)	1

1. In blender, on high speed, blend frozen strawberries, cranberry juice, lemon juice and rum until smooth.

2. Pour into a piña colada or old-fashioned glass and garnish with strawberry (or cranberries).

Makes 1 serving

Breezy Rouge

4	frozen strawberries	4
1/2 cup	cranberry juice	125 mL
1 1/2 oz	spiced rum	40 mL
2	ice cubes	2
3	frozen cranberries	3

1. In blender, on high speed, blend strawberries, cranberry juice, rum and ice until smooth.

2. Pour into a cocktail or wine glass and garnish with cranberries.

Cuban Punch

Makes 1 serving

½ tsp	freshly grated orange zest	2 mL
1 cup	orange juice	250 mL
½ cup	frozen strawberries	125 mL
½ cup	cubed pineapple	125 mL
2 oz	coconut or amber rum	50 mL
1	ice cube	1

1. In blender, on high speed, blend orange zest, orange juice, strawberries, pineapple, rum and ice until smooth.

2. Pour into a large stemmed punch glass.

Fruity Rum Mix-Up

Makes 1 serving

Garnish this fruity and slushy purple "Mix-Up" with a strawberry, peach wedge or cherry.

2	ice cubes	2
3	frozen strawberries	3
½ cup	black cherry or raspberry juice	125 mL
½ cup	frozen sliced peaches or nectarines	125 mL
¼ cup	pitted sweet cherries	50 mL
¼ cup	frozen raspberries	50 mL
1 ½ oz	amber or white rum	40 mL
½ oz	peach or apricot brandy	15 mL

1. In blender, pulse ice until crushed. On high speed, blend in strawberries, black cherry juice, peaches, cherries, raspberries, rum and brandy until slushy.

2. Pour into a piña colada or highball glass.

Makes 1 serving

Fruit Basket

TIP

Look for pear nectar or juice in bottles or cartons in the fruit juice section of well-stocked supermarkets and health food stores.

½ cup	frozen diced ripe mango	125 mL
2 tbsp	pear nectar or juice (see tip, at left)	25 mL
2 tbsp	apple cider or apple juice	25 mL
1 tsp	chopped crystallized ginger	5 mL
1 oz	amber rum	25 mL
1 oz	orange liqueur	25 mL
1	ice cube	1
1	slice orange	1
1	maraschino cherry (optional)	1

1. In blender, on high speed, blend mango, pear nectar, apple cider, ginger, rum, orange liqueur and ice until smooth.

2. Pour into an old-fashioned glass and garnish with orange slice and cherry, if desired.

Makes 1 serving

Shark Attack

¼ cup	frozen orange juice concentrate	50 mL
4 tsp	freshly squeezed lime juice	20 mL
2 oz	amber rum	50 mL
½ oz	orange liqueur	15 mL
4	ice cubes	4
1 tbsp	grenadine	15 mL

1. In blender, on high speed, blend orange juice concentrate, lime juice, rum, orange liqueur and ice until slushy.

2. Pour into a highball glass and top with grenadine.

Asian Blossom

This beautiful blend of fruit flavors can be garnished with a fresh or drained canned lichee, a cape gooseberry or a thin slice of Asian pear.

¼ cup	passion fruit juice	50 mL
¼ cup	pear nectar or juice (see tip, page 101)	50 mL
1 ½ oz	vanilla rum or rum	40 mL
½ oz	lichee liqueur	15 mL
2	ice cubes	2

1. In blender, on high speed, blend passion fruit juice, pear nectar, rum, lichee liqueur and ice until smooth.

2. Pour into a large martini glass.

Rum Alexander

¼ cup	light (5%) cream	50 mL
1 oz	vanilla rum	25 mL
1 oz	orange liqueur	25 mL
2	ice cubes	2
1	slice orange or twist orange rind	1

1. In blender, on high speed, blend cream, rum, orange liqueur and ice until smooth.

2. Pour into a martini glass and garnish with orange slice or twist.

Makes 1 serving

Jamaican Dirty Banana

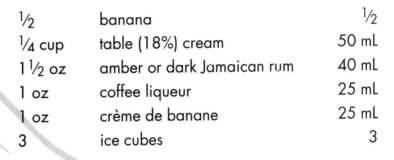

½	banana	½
¼ cup	table (18%) cream	50 mL
1 ½ oz	amber or dark Jamaican rum	40 mL
1 oz	coffee liqueur	25 mL
1 oz	crème de banane	25 mL
3	ice cubes	3

1. In blender, on high speed, blend banana, cream, rum, coffee liqueur, crème de banane and ice until smooth.

2. Pour into a highball glass.

Makes 1 serving

All over Taiwan, non-alcoholic papaya shakes are enjoyed. Why not spike it up?

Spiked Taiwan Papaya Shake

1 cup	cubed peeled and seeded papaya	250 mL
3 tbsp	sweetened condensed milk	45 mL
1 tsp	freshly squeezed lime juice	5 mL
2 oz	white or amber rum	50 mL
3	ice cubes	3

1. In blender, on high speed, blend papaya, condensed milk, lime juice, rum and ice until smooth.

2. Pour into a tall glass.

Filipino Avocado Dream

Makes 1 serving

In the Philippines, avocados grow abundantly. They are eaten only as dessert, with sweetened condensed milk over grated ice (thus the inspiration for this yummy drink).

½	avocado, peeled	½
2 tbsp	sweetened condensed milk	25 mL
2 oz	white or amber rum	50 mL
3	ice cubes	3

1. In blender, on high speed, blend avocado, condensed milk, rum and ice until smooth.

2. Pour into an old-fashioned glass.

Tom and Jerry

Makes 1 serving

This warming (and nutritious) winter drink is much easier to make in the blender than with the traditional whisking method.

This recipe contains a raw egg. If the food safety of raw eggs is a concern for you, use the pasteurized liquid whole egg instead.

1	egg, separated (or ¼ cup/50 mL pasteurized liquid whole egg)	1
1 tbsp	confectioner's (icing) sugar	15 mL
1½ oz	dark rum	40 mL
1½ oz	brandy	40 mL
½ cup	boiling water (approx.)	125 mL
Pinch	freshly ground nutmeg	Pinch

1. In blender, on high speed, beat egg white until frothy. Add yolk and continue blending until very frothy. (Or blend pasteurized liquid whole egg until very frothy.) Blend in rum and brandy just until mixed.

2. Pour into a mug and top with boiling water. Sprinkle with nutmeg.

Makes 1 serving

Coffee-Rum

Coffee and rum are a match made in tropical heaven. For a mocha flavor, dust the drink with a little grated semisweet chocolate. If desired, you can replace the coffee liqueur with a shot of strong espresso coffee.

1 oz	amber rum	25 mL
½ oz	coffee liqueur	15 mL
½ oz	Irish cream liqueur	15 mL
2	ice cubes	2

1. In blender, on high speed, blend rum, coffee liqueur, Irish cream liqueur and ice until smooth.

2. Pour into a martini or cocktail glass.

Makes 1 serving

Cuban Morning

¼ cup	brewed espresso coffee, cooled	50 mL
1 tbsp	whipping (35%) cream	15 mL
	Confectioner's (icing) sugar	
1 ½ oz	amber rum (preferably aged Cuban rum)	40 mL
2	ice cubes	2

1. In blender, on high speed, blend coffee, whipping cream, sugar to taste, rum and ice until smooth.

2. Pour into an old-fashioned glass or a coffee cup.

Berry Mojito

2 tbsp	freshly squeezed lime juice	25 mL
2 tbsp	Simple Syrup (see page 5)	25 mL
1 tbsp	chopped fresh mint	15 mL
1 ½ oz	white or amber rum	40 mL
½ oz	raspberry liqueur or framboise	15 mL
3	ice cubes	3
3	fresh raspberries (or 1 slice lime)	3

1. In blender, on high speed, blend lime juice, Simple Syrup, mint, rum, raspberry liqueur and ice until smooth.

2. Pour into an old-fashioned glass and garnish with raspberries (or lime slice).

Pomegranate Mojito

TIP

Pomegranate cocktails can be made with purchased pomegranate juice or with freshly squeezed juice. To juice a pomegranate, cut it in half and use a citrus reamer or juicer; strain. One large pomegranate will yield about ½ cup (125 mL) juice.

¼ cup	pomegranate juice (see tip, at left)	50 mL
1 tbsp	Simple Syrup (see page 5)	15 mL
1 tbsp	chopped fresh mint	15 mL
1 ½ oz	white rum	40 mL
3	ice cubes	3
¼ cup	chilled soda water	50 mL
1	sprig fresh mint	1
1	slice lime	1

1. In blender, on high speed, blend pomegranate juice, Simple Syrup, chopped mint, rum and ice until smooth.

2. Pour into an old-fashioned or highball glass and top with soda. Garnish with mint sprig and lime slice.

Makes 1 serving

Pineapple Fizz

When blended, pineapple fizzes — almost as if an egg white was added.

1 cup	cubed pineapple	250 mL
2 tsp	freshly squeezed lime juice	10 mL
1 ½ tsp	confectioner's (icing) sugar	7 mL
2 oz	white or amber rum	50 mL
2	ice cubes	2
2 tbsp	soda water or seltzer (approx.)	25 mL

1. In blender, on high speed, blend pineapple, lime juice, sugar, rum and ice until smooth.

2. Pour into a highball glass and top with soda.

Makes 1 serving

Citrus Rum Fizz

This recipe contains a raw egg white. If the food safety of raw eggs is a concern for you, use the pasteurized liquid egg white instead.

1	egg white (or 2 tbsp/25 mL pasteurized liquid egg white)	1
¼ cup	orange juice	50 mL
2 tbsp	freshly squeezed lime juice	25 mL
1 tbsp	freshly squeezed lemon juice	15 mL
1 ½ tsp	confectioner's (icing) sugar	7 mL
2 oz	amber rum	50 mL
2	ice cubes	2
2 tbsp	soda water or seltzer (approx.)	25 mL

1. In blender, on high speed, blend egg white, orange, lime and lemon juices, sugar, rum and ice until smooth.

2. Pour into a highball glass and top with soda.

Makes 1 serving

Cranberry Cooler

¼ cup	frozen cranberry cocktail concentrate	50 mL
2 oz	white rum	50 mL
1 oz	orange liqueur	25 mL
6	ice cubes	6
¼ cup	tonic water	50 mL
1	lime wedge	1

1. In blender, on high speed, blend cranberry cocktail concentrate, rum, orange liqueur and ice until smooth.

2. Pour into a highball glass and top with tonic water. Garnish with lime wedge.

Makes 1 serving

Julian's Frozen Trailer

This one's for fans of the Canadian television phenomenon Trailer Park Boys.

1 ½ cups	chilled cola	375 mL
2 ½ oz	white rum	65 mL
1	lime wedge	1

1. Pour half of the cola into small ice cube trays; freeze.

2. In blender, on high speed, blend cola cubes and rum until slushy.

3. Pour into an old-fashioned glass and top with remaining cola. Garnish with lime wedge.

Makes 1 serving

The tea picks you up, and the rum mellows you down.

Tropical Spiced Tea

⅓ cup	chilled strong orange pekoe tea	75 mL
2 tsp	freshly squeezed lemon juice	10 mL
1½ oz	spiced rum	40 mL
½ oz	orange liqueur	15 mL
3	ice cubes	3
¼ cup	chilled ginger ale	50 mL
1	slice lemon	1

1. In blender, on high speed, blend tea, lemon juice, rum, orange liqueur and ice until smooth.

2. Pour into a highball glass and top with ginger ale. Garnish with lemon slice.

Makes 1 serving

Mai Tai Freezie

¼ cup	lime sorbet	50 mL
2 tsp	grenadine	10 mL
1 tsp	orgeat (almond) syrup	5 mL
1½ oz	amber rum	40 mL
1 oz	orange liqueur	25 mL
1	slice orange	1
1	maraschino cherry (optional)	1

1. In blender, on high speed, blend sorbet, grenadine, orgeat syrup, rum and orange liqueur until smooth.

2. Pour into a piña colada glass and garnish with orange slice and cherry, if desired.

Makes 1 serving

Knickerbocker

The Knickerbocker is a classic cocktail developed in 1862; here is a blender variation.

¼ cup	raspberry sorbet	50 mL
1 tbsp	freshly squeezed lemon juice	15 mL
2 oz	amber rum	50 mL
½ oz	orange liqueur	15 mL
1	ice cube	1
3	fresh raspberries	3
1	slice lemon	1

1. In blender, on high speed, blend sorbet, lemon juice, rum, orange liqueur and ice until smooth.

2. Pour into an old-fashioned glass. Skewer raspberries and lemon and garnish drink.

Makes 1 serving

Golden Passion

TIP

Look for passion fruit nectar or juice in bottles or cartons in the fruit juice section of well-stocked supermarkets and health food stores.

½	frozen ripe banana	½
¼ cup	orange juice	50 mL
¼ cup	passion fruit nectar or juice (see tip, at left)	50 mL
¼ cup	vanilla frozen yogurt or ice cream	50 mL
2 oz	vanilla or amber rum	50 mL
2	ice cubes	2
1	slice banana	1
1	maraschino cherry (optional)	1

1. In blender, on high speed, blend frozen banana, orange juice, passion fruit nectar, frozen yogurt, rum and ice until smooth.

2. Pour into a piña colada or old-fashioned glass and garnish with banana slice and cherry, if desired.

Makes 1 serving

Sunburst

This creamy orange cocktail tastes like fruit punch. For an attractive garnish, alternate cubes of fresh mango and raspberries on a skewer.

6	frozen raspberries	6
1/2 cup	frozen diced ripe mango	125 mL
1/4 cup	apple cider or apple juice	50 mL
1/4 cup	vanilla frozen yogurt or ice cream	50 mL
2 oz	amber rum	50 mL

1. In blender, on high speed, blend raspberries, mango, apple cider, frozen yogurt and rum until smooth.

2. Pour into a piña colada or old-fashioned glass.

Makes 1 serving

Apple Sundae

1/2 cup	apple cider	125 mL
1/2 cup	vanilla or caramel ice cream	125 mL
1 oz	vanilla or amber rum	25 mL
1/2 oz	almond liqueur	15 mL
1/2 oz	cinnamon schnapps	15 mL
1	cinnamon stick or slice apple	1

1. In blender, on high speed, blend apple cider, ice cream, rum, almond liqueur and cinnamon schnapps until smooth.

2. Pour into an old-fashioned glass and garnish with cinnamon stick or apple slice.

Makes 1 serving

TIP

If you don't have caramel ice cream, you can substitute an equal amount of vanilla ice cream and add 2 tbsp (25 mL) caramel syrup.

Frozen Caramel Pineapple

½ cup	caramel ice cream (see tip, at left)	125 mL
¼ cup	pineapple juice	50 mL
2 oz	vanilla rum or rum	50 mL
1	pineapple wedge (optional)	1
1 tsp	caramel syrup (optional)	5 mL

1. In blender, on high speed, blend ice cream, pineapple juice and rum until smooth.

2. Pour into a wine or piña colada glass. Garnish with pineapple wedge and/or drizzle with syrup, if desired.

Makes 1 serving

Post-prandial Strawberry Shake

6	fresh or frozen strawberries	6
¼ cup	vanilla ice cream	50 mL
2 oz	white or amber rum	50 mL
½ oz	orange liqueur	15 mL
1	fresh strawberry (optional)	1

1. In blender, on high speed, blend strawberries, ice cream, rum and orange liqueur until smooth.

2. Pour into an old-fashioned glass and garnish with strawberry, if desired.

Makes 1 serving

Scorpion

The luscious and fruity sweetness of this cocktail takes away all the sting of the alcohol.

1	frozen ripe banana	1
2 tbsp	vanilla ice cream	25 mL
2 tbsp	creamed coconut	25 mL
1 ½ oz	amber or white rum	40 mL
½ oz	brandy	15 mL
1	maraschino cherry	1

1. In blender, on high speed, blend banana, ice cream, creamed coconut, rum and brandy until smooth.

2. Pour into a large martini or old-fashioned glass and garnish with cherry.

Makes 1 serving

Bananas Foster

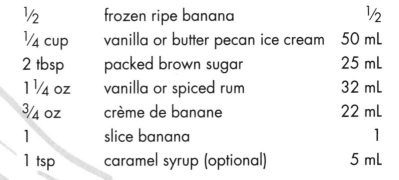

½	frozen ripe banana	½
¼ cup	vanilla or butter pecan ice cream	50 mL
2 tbsp	packed brown sugar	25 mL
1 ¼ oz	vanilla or spiced rum	32 mL
¾ oz	crème de banane	22 mL
1	slice banana	1
1 tsp	caramel syrup (optional)	5 mL

1. In blender, on high speed, blend frozen banana, ice cream, brown sugar, rum and crème de banane until smooth.

2. Pour into a piña colada or old-fashioned glass, garnish with banana slice and drizzle with syrup, if desired.

Banana Boat

½	frozen ripe banana	½
¼ cup	vanilla ice cream	50 mL
2 tsp	freshly squeezed lemon juice	10 mL
1 oz	amber or vanilla rum	25 mL
¼ oz	crème de banane	7 mL
¼ oz	orange liqueur	7 mL
1	slice banana or orange	1

1. In blender, on high speed, blend frozen banana, ice cream, lemon juice, rum, crème de banane and orange liqueur until smooth.

2. Pour into a piña colada or old-fashioned glass and garnish with banana or orange slice.

Banana Splish-Splash

1	banana	1
½ cup	cubed pineapple	125 mL
¼ cup	orange juice	50 mL
¼ cup	vanilla ice cream	50 mL
1½ oz	amber or dark rum	40 mL
½ oz	coconut rum	15 mL
3	ice cubes	3

1. In blender, on high speed, blend banana, pineapple, orange juice, ice cream, amber and coconut rums and ice until slushy.

2. Pour into a milkshake glass or a tall stemmed punch glass.

Malibu Monkey Milkshake

¼ cup	chocolate ice cream	50 mL
1 oz	coconut rum	25 mL
1 oz	crème de banane	25 mL
4	ice cubes	4
1 tsp	grated bittersweet chocolate (optional)	5 mL

1. In blender, on high speed, blend ice cream, rum, crème de banane and ice until smooth.

2. Pour into an old-fashioned or highball glass and sprinkle with chocolate, if desired.

Banana-Orangutan

1	frozen ripe banana	1
¼ cup	vanilla ice cream	50 mL
2 tbsp	frozen orange juice concentrate	25 mL
1 oz	vanilla or amber rum	25 mL
½ oz	crème de banane	15 mL
1	slice orange	1

1. In blender, on high speed, blend banana, ice cream, orange juice concentrate, rum and crème de banane until smooth.

2. Pour into a piña colada or old-fashioned glass and garnish with orange slice.

Makes 1 serving

Cocobananarama

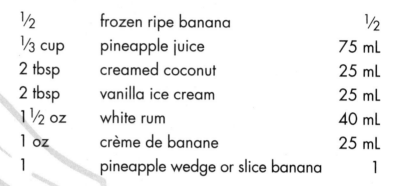

½	frozen ripe banana	½
⅓ cup	pineapple juice	75 mL
2 tbsp	creamed coconut	25 mL
2 tbsp	vanilla ice cream	25 mL
1 ½ oz	white rum	40 mL
1 oz	crème de banane	25 mL
1	pineapple wedge or slice banana	1

1. In blender, on high speed, blend frozen banana, pineapple juice, creamed coconut, ice cream, rum and crème de banane until smooth.

2. Pour into a piña colada or old-fashioned glass and garnish with pineapple wedge or banana slice.

Makes 1 serving

Gaelic Coconut

⅓ cup	vanilla ice cream	75 mL
2 tbsp	creamed coconut	25 mL
1 oz	coconut or white rum	25 mL
1 oz	Irish cream liqueur	25 mL
3 tbsp	chilled soda water	45 mL
1 tsp	toasted coconut (optional)	5 mL

1. In blender, on high speed, blend ice cream, creamed coconut, rum and Irish cream liqueur until smooth.

2. Pour into a piña colada glass and top with soda. Sprinkle with toasted coconut, if desired.

Makes 1 serving

This tropical dessert cocktail can be sprinkled with a little toasted coconut to add to the coconut flavor.

Cocobanana Cream Pie

½	frozen ripe banana	½
⅓ cup	vanilla ice cream	75 mL
2 tbsp	creamed coconut	25 mL
1 tbsp	mascarpone or cream cheese	15 mL
2 oz	vanilla or amber rum	50 mL
2	ice cubes	2
1	slice banana	1

1. In blender, on high speed, blend frozen banana, ice cream, creamed coconut, mascarpone, rum and ice until smooth.

2. Pour into a piña colada or old-fashioned glass and garnish with banana slice.

Makes 1 serving

Vanilla Choco-Blaster

¾ cup	chocolate ice cream	175 mL
¾ cup	milk or light (5%) cream	175 mL
1 oz	vanilla rum or rum	25 mL
1 oz	white crème de cacao	25 mL
	Grated semisweet chocolate	

1. In blender, on high speed, blend ice cream, milk, rum and crème de cacao until smooth.

2. Pour into a piña colada or old-fashioned glass and sprinkle with chocolate.

Makes 1 serving

Choco-Mint Blaster

¾ cup	chocolate-mint ice cream	175 mL
¾ cup	milk or light (5%) cream	175 mL
1 oz	vanilla rum or rum	25 mL
½ oz	white crème de cacao	15 mL
½ oz	white crème de menthe	15 mL
1	sprig fresh mint	1

1. In blender, on high speed, blend ice cream, milk, rum, crème de cacao and crème de menthe until smooth.

2. Pour into a piña colada or old-fashioned glass and garnish with mint sprig.

Makes 1 serving

Serve this drink as a dessert.

Rum 'n' Raisin

2 tbsp	raisins	25 mL
2 oz	spiced rum	50 mL
½ cup	vanilla ice cream	125 mL
2 tbsp	caramel sauce or syrup	25 mL
1	cinnamon stick	1

1. In a small bowl, soak raisins in rum for 30 minutes.

2. In blender, on high speed, blend raisin-rum mixture, ice cream and caramel sauce until raisins are very finely chopped but not puréed.

3. Pour into an old-fashioned glass and garnish with cinnamon stick.

Makes 1 serving

Vanilla Nutty Nog

1/2 cup	prepared eggnog	125 mL
1/4 cup	vanilla ice cream	50 mL
1 1/2 oz	vanilla rum	40 mL
1/2 oz	almond liqueur	15 mL
2	ice cubes	2
Pinch	ground nutmeg or cinnamon	Pinch

1. In blender, on high speed, blend eggnog, ice cream, rum, almond liqueur and ice until smooth.

2. Pour into an old-fashioned or wine glass and sprinkle with nutmeg or cinnamon.

Makes 1 serving

Nutty Iced Coffee

1/2 cup	vanilla or coffee ice cream	125 mL
1/4 cup	chilled strong coffee or espresso	50 mL
1 oz	amber rum	25 mL
1/2 oz	crème de cacao	15 mL
1/2 oz	hazelnut liqueur	15 mL
3	coffee beans or chocolate-coated coffee beans	3

1. In blender, on high speed, blend ice cream, coffee, rum, crème de cacao and hazelnut liqueur until smooth.

2. Pour into an old-fashioned glass and garnish with coffee beans.

Makes 1 serving

Coffee Cream

½ cup	coffee ice cream	125 mL
1 oz	vanilla or amber rum	25 mL
1 oz	Irish cream liqueur	25 mL
3	chocolate-covered coffee beans	3

1. In blender, on high speed, blend ice cream, rum and Irish cream liqueur until smooth.

2. Pour into an old-fashioned glass and top with coffee beans.

Makes 1 serving

Orange Coffee Cream

¼ cup	vanilla ice cream	50 mL
2 tbsp	frozen orange juice concentrate	25 mL
1 oz	amber or white rum	25 mL
½ oz	coffee liqueur	15 mL
½ oz	orange liqueur	15 mL
1	slice kumquat or orange	1

1. In blender, on high speed, blend ice cream, orange juice concentrate, rum, coffee liqueur and orange liqueur until smooth.

2. Pour into a large martini glass and garnish with kumquat or orange slice.

Makes 1 serving

Mocha Hum

¼ cup	vanilla or coffee ice cream	50 mL
¼ cup	light (5%) cream	50 mL
1 ½ oz	spiced or amber rum	40 mL
1 oz	coffee liqueur	25 mL

1. In blender, on high speed, blend ice cream, cream, rum and coffee liqueur until smooth.

2. Pour into an old-fashioned glass.

Makes 1 serving

Russian Cola

¼ cup	vanilla ice cream	50 mL
1 ½ oz	amber or white rum	40 mL
½ oz	coffee liqueur	15 mL
¼ cup	chilled cola	50 mL

1. In blender, on high speed, blend ice cream, rum and coffee liqueur until smooth.

2. Pour into a highball glass and top with cola.

gin

GIN ORIGINATED IN HOLLAND in the 16th century, when the chemist Dr. Franciscus Sylvius at the University of Leyden made an infusion of juniper berries in neutral grain spirits for medicinal purposes. He called in *genièvre* (French for "juniper berries"). Soon, a sweetened version of the drink became popular and was imported to Britain. The spirit flourished there and has since almost exclusively been associated with these isles. When we now speak of gin, we almost always mean English gin, a dry neutral spirit redistilled with the addition of juniper berries and other herbal and even floral elements ranging from bitter orange peel, coriander seed and cardamom to licorice root and angelica, among many others (each recipe guarded zealously by the distilleries). The mysterious, subtle, layered flavors of gin contribute to its success as a blending liquor, adding much depth and interest of flavor in a cocktail. Identify the gin whose flavors you like best, and that gin will also be your best bet in blending drinks.

Dutch-style gin, now generally referred to as genever, is a very potent and slightly sweet style of gin usually drunk chilled and straight up. Occasionally, it can add a special flavor to a mixed drink, but it remains an outsider at the cocktail bar.

GIN RECIPES

Orange Martini

3 tbsp	freshly squeezed orange juice	45 mL
1 oz	gin	25 mL
½ oz	dry vermouth	15 mL
½ oz	orange liqueur	15 mL
Dash	angostura bitters	Dash
2	ice cubes	2
1	twist orange rind	1

1. In blender, on high speed, blend orange juice, gin, vermouth, orange liqueur, bitters and ice until smooth.

2. Pour into a martini glass and garnish with orange twist.

Hint o' Raspberry Martini

3	frozen raspberries	3
1 tbsp	freshly squeezed lemon juice	15 mL
2 tsp	Simple Syrup (see page 5)	10 mL
1 oz	gin	25 mL
1 oz	raspberry vodka	25 mL
2	ice cubes	2
1	fresh raspberry	1
1	twist lemon rind	1

1. In blender, on high speed, blend frozen raspberries, lemon juice, Simple Syrup, gin, vodka and ice until smooth.

2. Pour into a martini glass and garnish with raspberry and lemon twist.

Makes 1 serving

Raspberry Martini

¼ cup	frozen unsweetened raspberries	50 mL
2 oz	gin or vodka	50 mL
1 oz	orange liqueur	25 mL
2 dashes	angostura bitters	2 dashes

1. In blender, on high speed, blend raspberries, gin, orange liqueur and bitters until smooth.

2. Strain through a fine sieve into a martini glass.

Makes 1 serving

Pineapple Basiltini

⅓ cup	frozen cubed pineapple	75 mL
1 tbsp	chopped fresh basil	15 mL
2 tsp	freshly squeezed lemon juice	10 mL
2 tsp	Simple Syrup (see page 5)	10 mL
1 oz	gin	25 mL
1 oz	vodka	25 mL
1	twist lemon rind	1

1. In blender, on high speed, blend pineapple, basil, lemon juice, Simple Syrup, gin and vodka until smooth.

2. Strain through a fine sieve into a martini or cocktail glass and garnish with lemon twist.

Watermelon and Basil Martini

5	fresh basil leaves	5
1 cup	frozen cubed seedless watermelon	250 mL
Pinch	salt	Pinch
2 oz	gin	50 mL
Dash	angostura bitters	Dash

1. In blender, on high speed, blend basil, watermelon, salt, gin and bitters until smooth.

2. Strain through a fine sieve into a martini glass.

Pink Gin Whizz

1 tsp	confectioner's (icing) sugar	5 mL
1 tsp	freshly squeezed lemon juice	5 mL
2 oz	gin	50 mL
4 dashes	angostura bitters	4 dashes
2	ice cubes	2

1. In blender, on high speed, blend icing sugar, lemon juice, gin, bitters and ice until ice is well crushed.

2. Pour into an old-fashioned glass.

Apple Gin Blossom

4	frozen raspberries	4
1/4 cup	apple cider or apple juice	50 mL
4 tsp	elderflower syrup (see tip, at left)	20 mL
2 oz	gin	50 mL
1	thin slice apple	1

1. In blender, on high speed, blend raspberries, apple cider, elderflower syrup and gin until smooth.

2. Strain through a fine sieve into a large martini or wine glass and garnish with apple slice.

Pineapple Gin Blossom

1/4 cup	pineapple juice	50 mL
1 1/2 oz	gin	40 mL
1/2 oz	orange liqueur	15 mL
2	ice cubes	2
1	pineapple wedge	1

1. In blender, on high speed, blend pineapple juice, gin, orange liqueur and ice until smooth.

2. Pour into a piña colada glass and garnish with pineapple wedge.

Orange Gin Blossom

3 tbsp	freshly squeezed orange juice	45 mL
1 tbsp	freshly squeezed lime juice	15 mL
1 ½ oz	gin	40 mL
½ oz	orange liqueur	15 mL
2	ice cubes	2
1	slice orange or twist orange rind	1

1. In blender, on high speed, blend orange juice, lime juice, gin, orange liqueur and ice until smooth.

2. Pour into a piña colada glass and garnish with orange slice or twist.

Red Lion

This orangey cocktail is adapted from an original from the early 1930s.

3 tbsp	freshly squeezed orange juice	45 mL
1 tbsp	freshly squeezed lemon juice	15 mL
1 oz	gin	25 mL
1 oz	orange liqueur	25 mL
2	ice cubes	2
¼ tsp	grenadine	1 mL
1	twist orange rind	1

1. In blender, on high speed, blend orange juice, lemon juice, gin, orange liqueur and ice until smooth.

2. Pour into a large martini or wine glass, drizzle with grenadine and garnish with orange twist.

Makes 1 serving

Big Orange Ben

1/3 cup	orange juice	75 mL
1 tbsp	orange marmalade	15 mL
1 oz	gin	25 mL
1 oz	Pimm's No. 1 liqueur	25 mL
2	ice cubes	2
1	slice cucumber	1

1. In blender, on high speed, blend orange juice, orange marmalade, gin, Pimm's and ice until smooth.

2. Strain through a fine sieve into an old-fashioned glass and garnish with cucumber.

Makes 1 serving

Paradise

If paradise were a color, it would surely be the pinkish-orange of this cocktail.

2 tbsp	orange or mango juice	25 mL
2 tsp	grenadine	10 mL
1 oz	gin	25 mL
1 oz	apricot brandy	25 mL
2	ice cubes	2
1	twist orange rind	1

1. In blender, on high speed, blend orange juice, grenadine, gin, brandy and ice until smooth.

2. Pour into a martini glass and garnish with orange twist.

Makes 1 serving

Winter Greyhound

This is the blender version of the well-known Florida grapefruit cocktail.

¼ cup	frozen grapefruit juice concentrate	50 mL
2 oz	gin	50 mL
6	ice cubes	6

1. In blender, on high speed, blend grapefruit juice concentrate, gin and ice until slushy.

2. Pour into a highball glass.

Makes 1 serving

Pink Greyhound

¼ cup	frozen pink grapefruit juice concentrate	50 mL
2 oz	gin	50 mL
2 dashes	angostura bitters	2 dashes
6	ice cubes	6

1. In blender, on high speed, blend grapefruit juice concentrate, gin, bitters and ice until slushy.

2. Pour into a highball glass.

Makes 1 serving

TIP

To toast coriander seeds, fry in a dry skillet over medium-low heat until seeds are fragrant and wiggle on the hot surface.

Coriander Pink Grapefruit

¼ cup	pink grapefruit juice	50 mL
1 tsp	chopped fresh mint	5 mL
¼ tsp	coriander seeds, toasted (see tip, at left)	1 mL
2 oz	gin or lemon gin	50 mL
1	ice cube	1
	Lime juice, for rimming	
	Granulated sugar, for rimming	
1	sprig fresh mint	1

1. In blender, on high speed, blend grapefruit juice, chopped mint, coriander seeds, gin and ice until smooth.

2. Pour into a martini glass rimmed with lime juice and sugar. Garnish with mint sprig.

Makes 1 serving

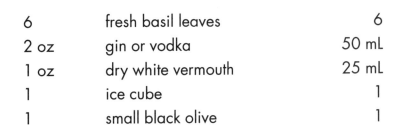

Green Goddess

6	fresh basil leaves	6
2 oz	gin or vodka	50 mL
1 oz	dry white vermouth	25 mL
1	ice cube	1
1	small black olive	1

1. In blender, on high speed, blend basil, gin, vermouth and ice until smooth.

2. Strain through a fine sieve into a martini glass and garnish with olive.

Makes 1 serving

Gin Passion

¼ cup	freshly squeezed orange juice	50 mL
½ tsp	grenadine	2 mL
1 oz	gin	25 mL
1 oz	passion fruit liqueur	25 mL
2	ice cubes	2
1	slice orange	1

1. In blender, on high speed, blend orange juice, grenadine, gin, passion fruit liqueur and ice until smooth.

2. Pour into an old-fashioned glass and garnish with orange slice.

Makes 1 serving

Besides the traditional Pimm's Cup, not too many drinks make use of cucumber. Serve this one to friends some summer evening and make a splash.

Mint Cucumber Refresher

½ cup	chopped seeded peeled cucumber	125 mL
1 tbsp	chopped fresh mint	15 mL
1 tsp	freshly grated gingerroot	5 mL
2 oz	gin	50 mL
3	ice cubes	3
1	slice cucumber	1
1	sprig fresh mint	1

1. In blender, on high speed, blend cucumber, chopped mint, ginger, gin and ice until smooth.

2. Strain through a fine sieve into an old-fashioned glass and garnish with cucumber slice and mint sprig.

Gin Mint Julep

Makes 1 serving

Although the original mint julep is made with bourbon, as befits its Southern origin, mint and gin are a wonderful pairing too.

2 tbsp	freshly squeezed lime juice	25 mL
2 tbsp	Simple Syrup (see page 5)	25 mL
1 tbsp	chopped fresh mint	15 mL
2 oz	gin	50 mL
3	ice cubes	3
¼ cup	chilled soda water	50 mL
1	sprig fresh mint	1

1. In blender, on high speed, blend lime juice, Simple Syrup, chopped mint, gin and ice until smooth.

2. Pour into a piña colada or old-fashioned glass and top with soda. Garnish with mint sprig.

Après les Huîtres

Makes 1 serving

For a version of this drink that is more like a digestive — perfect after a meal of oysters — add a few dashes of angostura bitters. This drink can also be called a Tom Collins Slushy.

2 tbsp	frozen lemonade concentrate	25 mL
1 tbsp	Simple Syrup (see page 5)	15 mL
2 oz	gin	50 mL
1	ice cube	1
¼ cup	soda water or seltzer	50 mL
1	lemon wedge	1

1. In blender, on high speed, blend lemonade concentrate, Simple Syrup, gin and ice until smooth.

2. Pour into a highball glass and top with soda. Garnish with lemon wedge.

Summer Rose

Garnish with fresh raspberries, strawberries or a sprig of mint.

4	frozen raspberries	4
3	frozen strawberries	3
¼ cup	cranberry juice	50 mL
2 tsp	Simple Syrup (see page 5)	10 mL
1 tsp	rosewater	5 mL
1 oz	gin	25 mL
1 oz	passion fruit liqueur	25 mL
2	ice cubes	2

1. In blender, on high speed, blend raspberries, strawberries, cranberry juice, Simple Syrup, rosewater, gin, passion fruit liqueur and ice until smooth.

2. Strain through a fine sieve into a piña colada or old-fashioned glass.

Gin Fizz

This recipe contains a raw egg white. If the food safety of raw eggs is a concern for you, use the pasteurized liquid egg white instead.

1	egg white (or 2 tbsp/25 mL pasteurized liquid egg white)	1
2 tbsp	freshly squeezed lemon juice	25 mL
1 tbsp	whipping (35%) cream	15 mL
1½ tsp	confectioner's (icing) sugar	7 mL
2 oz	gin	50 mL
2	ice cubes	2
2 tbsp	soda water or seltzer (approx.)	25 mL

1. In blender, on high speed, blend egg white, lemon juice, whipping cream, sugar, gin and ice until smooth and frothy.

2. Pour into a highball glass and top with soda.

Makes 1 serving

Sloe Gin Fizz

Sloe gin is fortified with sloes — a plum-like fruit of the blackthorn tree — rather than juniper berries and spices. It is especially popular in Holland and, in North America, it is most appreciated in Quebec.

¼ cup	lemon sorbet	50 mL
2 oz	sloe gin	50 mL
½ cup	chilled soda water	125 mL
½ tsp	grenadine	2 mL
1	lemon slice or wedge	1

1. In blender, on high speed, blend sorbet and sloe gin until smooth.

2. Pour into a piña colada or old-fashioned glass, top with soda and drizzle with grenadine. Garnish with lemon slice or wedge.

Makes 1 serving

Citrus Gin Fizz

Gin fizzes are traditionally served in the late morning during summertime (although we don't officially advocate morning imbibing). Being morning drinks, most fizzes include citrus, but ours has three kinds for your health!

2 tbsp	freshly squeezed lemon juice	25 mL
1 tbsp	freshly squeezed lime juice	15 mL
1 tbsp	Simple Syrup (see page 5)	15 mL
2 oz	gin	50 mL
½ oz	orange liqueur	15 mL
2	ice cubes	2
¼ cup	soda water	50 mL
1	slice orange, lemon and/or lime	1
1	maraschino cherry	1

1. In blender, on high speed, blend lemon juice, lime juice, Simple Syrup, gin, orange liqueur and ice until smooth.

2. Pour into a highball glass and top with soda. Skewer citrus slice(s) and cherry and garnish drink.

Royal Fizz

This recipe contains a raw egg. If the food safety of raw eggs is a concern for you, use the pasteurized liquid whole egg instead.

1	egg (or ¼ cup/50 mL pasteurized liquid whole egg)	1
2 tbsp	freshly squeezed lemon juice	25 mL
1 tsp	confectioner's (icing) sugar	5 mL
2 oz	gin	50 mL
2	ice cubes	2
2 tbsp	soda water or seltzer (approx.)	25 mL

1. In blender, on high speed, blend egg, lemon juice, sugar, gin and ice until smooth and frothy.

2. Pour into a highball glass and top with soda.

Elderflower Fizz

TIP

Elderflower syrup is available at specialty and gourmet shops. If you can't find it, substitute elderflower soda water or elderflower mineral water, available at many grocery stores.

2 tbsp	elderflower syrup (see tip, at left)	25 mL
2 tbsp	freshly squeezed lemon juice	25 mL
2 tsp	liquid honey	10 mL
2 oz	gin or lemon gin	50 mL
3	ice cubes	3
¼ cup	chilled soda water	50 mL
1	slice lemon	1

1. In blender, on high speed, blend elderflower syrup, lemon juice, honey, gin and ice until smooth.

2. Pour into a highball glass and top with soda. Garnish with lemon slice.

Frozen Lemon Gin

This lemony cocktail is equally good with bourbon instead of gin. If you are lucky enough to have a lemon tree in bloom, garnish the drink with a lemon blossom.

3	ice cubes	3
1/4 cup	frozen lemonade concentrate	50 mL
2 tbsp	freshly squeezed lemon juice	25 mL
2 oz	gin	50 mL
1	twist lemon rind	1

1. In blender, pulse ice and lemonade concentrate until ice is crushed. On high speed, blend in lemon juice and gin until slushy.

2. Pour into a wine or martini glass and garnish with lemon twist.

Citrus Blush

1/4 cup	orange juice	50 mL
2 tbsp	frozen limeade concentrate	25 mL
2 tsp	grenadine	10 mL
2 oz	gin	50 mL
2	ice cubes	2
1	twist orange or lime rind	1

1. In blender, on high speed, blend orange juice, limeade concentrate, grenadine, gin and ice until slushy.

2. Pour into an old-fashioned glass and garnish with orange or lime twist.

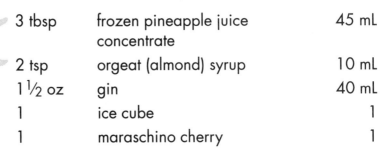

Makes 1 serving

Nutty Pineapple

3 tbsp	frozen pineapple juice concentrate	45 mL
2 tsp	orgeat (almond) syrup	10 mL
1½ oz	gin	40 mL
1	ice cube	1
1	maraschino cherry	1

1. In blender, on high speed, blend pineapple juice concentrate, orgeat syrup, gin and ice until smooth.

2. Pour into a martini glass and garnish with cherry.

Makes 1 serving

The orange hues and flavor of this cocktail really scream out "Summer!"

TIP

Look for peach nectar or juice in bottles or cartons in the fruit juice section of well-stocked supermarkets and health food stores.

Sunny Summer Gin

¼ cup	orange sorbet	50 mL
¼ cup	peach nectar or juice (see tip, at left)	50 mL
1 oz	orange gin or gin	25 mL
1 oz	peach schnapps	25 mL
1	twist orange rind	1

1. In blender, on high speed, blend sorbet, peach nectar, gin and peach schnapps until smooth.

2. Pour into a piña colada or old-fashioned glass and garnish with orange twist.

Garnet Gin Splash

¼ cup	orange sorbet	50 mL
1 ½ oz	red Dubonnet or red vermouth	40 mL
1 oz	gin or orange gin	25 mL
Dash	angostura bitters	Dash
1	slice orange	1

1. In blender, on high speed, blend sorbet, Dubonnet, gin and bitters until smooth.

2. Pour into an old-fashioned glass and garnish with orange slice.

Summer Pastels

¼ cup	lemon sorbet	50 mL
¼ cup	pink grapefruit juice	50 mL
1 oz	gin	25 mL
1 oz	melon liqueur	25 mL
1	ice cube	1
1	melon ball, skewered (or 3 fresh raspberries)	1

1. In blender, on high speed, blend sorbet, grapefruit juice, gin, melon liqueur and ice until smooth.

2. Pour into a piña colada or old-fashioned glass and garnish with melon (or raspberries).

Makes 1 serving

The aperitif Negroni originated in Florence, Italy, and has remained a popular favorite for decades.

Variation

For an unsweetened Negroni Slushy, replace the sorbet with 3 ice cubes and add just a splash of soda water.

Negroni Slushy

¼ cup	lime sorbet	50 mL
1 oz	gin	25 mL
1 oz	Campari	25 mL
½ oz	dry red vermouth	15 mL
¼ cup	chilled soda water	50 mL
1	slice orange or lime	1

1. In blender, on high speed, blend sorbet, gin, Campari and vermouth until smooth.

2. Pour into a piña colada or old-fashioned glass and top with soda. Garnish with orange or lime slice.

Makes 1 serving

Sophisto-Gin

2 tbsp	lime sorbet	25 mL
1 oz	lime gin or gin	25 mL
½ oz	orange liqueur	15 mL
¼ oz	anise liqueur, such as Pernod, ouzo or anisette	7 mL
¼ oz	crème de menthe	7 mL
2	ice cubes	2
1	twist orange rind	1

1. In blender, on high speed, blend sorbet, gin, orange liqueur, anise liqueur, crème de menthe and ice until smooth.

2. Pour into a martini glass and garnish with orange twist.

White Cargo

This traditional drink is for those who cannot decide if they want a post-prandial ice cream or a drink.

| ¼ cup | vanilla ice cream | 50 mL |
| 2 oz | gin | 50 mL |

1. In blender, on high speed, blend ice cream and gin until smooth.

2. Pour into an old-fashioned glass.

Pink Frozen Lady

This recipe contains a raw egg white. If the food safety of raw eggs is a concern for you, use the pasteurized liquid egg white instead.

1	egg white (or 2 tbsp/25 mL pasteurized liquid egg white)	1
¼ cup	vanilla ice cream	50 mL
1 tsp	grenadine	5 mL
2 oz	gin	50 mL
½ oz	cherry brandy	15 mL
1	maraschino cherry	1

1. In blender, on high speed, blend egg white, ice cream, grenadine, gin and brandy until smooth.

2. Pour into a piña colada or old-fashioned glass and garnish with cherry.

whiskey, bourbon and Scotch

WHISKEY (or whisky, as it is spelled in Scotland and Canada) is basically distilled from a mash similar to that used in fermenting beer. It has been distilled for over 700 years in the British Isles. Whiskey is more complicated in variety than most other liquors, as it has been produced in many different areas of the English- and Gaelic-speaking world over the centuries. For our purposes, we are interested in specific flavors that affect the taste of the cocktail to be blended.

The major varieties of whiskey are Scotch whisky, Irish whiskey, bourbon, Tennessee whiskey, Canadian whisky and American whiskey. Scotch is made from barley malt smoked over open peat ovens, lending the whisky a decidedly smoky flavor. The liquor is then aged in old bourbon or sherry casks, resulting in a smooth and not-too-woody taste. Irish whiskey's flavor is sweeter and not at all smoky because the malt is roasted in closed kilns, as are the whiskies produced in North America. Bourbon and Tennessee whiskey are made primarily from corn and are aged in new charred-oak casks, resulting in a sweet, somewhat burnt taste. Most blended cocktails that call for amber or dark rum can be successfully made with bourbon, although the taste will be distinctly different. Tennessee whiskey is distinguished by its slow filtering through sugar maple charcoal, which lends it a unique, clean, yet sweet flavor. Although Canadian whisky is generally called "rye" in Canada, it can be made from a blend of grains, including wheat and corn, with wheat often being the main ingredient. This accounts for its generally light flavor. American blended whiskey is similar to Canadian whisky, but often has a fuller flavor and sometimes a harsher mouth-feel.

All of these whiskies are good for blending drinks, with the exception of many Scotches, especially single-malt Scotches, whose individual characteristics and generally smoky attributes make it difficult to meld well with other flavors.

Whiskey is also the base of a variety of liqueurs. Drambuie is made from Scotch, while Southern Comfort is made from American whiskey. Irish cream liqueur is a blend of cream and Irish whiskey.

WHISKEY, BOURBON AND SCOTCH RECIPES

Makes 1 serving

Stone Fence

This recipe was adapted from one created in 1902 by American bartender Charlie Paul.

¾ cup	apple cider or apple juice	175 mL
1 tbsp	freshly squeezed lemon juice	15 mL
2 tsp	grenadine	10 mL
2 oz	bourbon	50 mL
1	thin slice apple	1

1. Pour apple cider into small ice cube trays; freeze.

2. In blender, on high speed, blend apple cider cubes, lemon juice, grenadine and bourbon until smooth.

3. Pour into an old-fashioned glass and garnish with apple slice.

Makes 1 serving

Frozen Tennessee Manhattan

2 tbsp	orange juice	25 mL
1 oz	Tennessee whiskey	25 mL
½ oz	sweet red vermouth	15 mL
Dash	angostura bitters	Dash
2	ice cubes	2
1	maraschino cherry or twist lemon rind	1

1. In blender, on high speed, blend orange juice, whiskey, vermouth, bitters and ice until smooth.

2. Pour into a martini or cocktail glass and garnish with cherry or lemon twist.

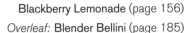

Blackberry Lemonade (page 156)
Overleaf: Blender Bellini (page 185)

Makes 1 serving

Highland Orange-Cranberry

¼ cup	freshly squeezed orange juice	50 mL
¼ cup	cranberry juice	50 mL
1 oz	Scotch whisky	25 mL
½ oz	orange liqueur	15 mL
½ oz	Drambuie	15 mL
3	ice cubes	3
1	slice orange	1

1. In blender, on high speed, blend orange juice, cranberry juice, Scotch, orange liqueur, Drambuie and ice until smooth.

2. Pour into an old-fashioned glass and garnish with orange slice.

Makes 1 serving

Glass o' Sunshine

½ cup	freshly squeezed orange juice	125 mL
⅓ cup	pineapple juice	75 mL
1 oz	rye whisky	25 mL
1 oz	vanilla or spiced rum	25 mL
3	ice cubes	3
1	pineapple wedge or slice orange	1

1. In blender, on high speed, blend orange juice, pineapple juice, whisky, rum and ice until smooth.

2. Pour into a piña colada or old-fashioned glass and garnish with pineapple wedge or orange slice.

Overleaf: **Apple Saketini** (page 190), **Kiwitini** (page 192), and **Peach Saketini** (page 190)

Golden Blue Margarita (page 167)

Makes 1 serving

Sour Cherries Jubilee

¼ cup	orange juice	50 mL
¼ cup	drained jarred sour cherries	50 mL
2 oz	rye whisky	50 mL
2 dashes	angostura bitters	2 dashes
2	ice cubes	2
1	maraschino cherry	1

1. In blender, on high speed, blend orange juice, sour cherries, whisky, bitters and ice until smooth.

2. Pour into an old-fashioned glass and garnish with maraschino cherry.

Makes 1 serving

Southern Saturday Night

¼ cup	cranberry juice	50 mL
1 ½ oz	bourbon	40 mL
½ oz	almond liqueur	15 mL
2	ice cubes	2
1	maraschino cherry (or 3 frozen cranberries)	1

1. In blender, on high speed, blend cranberry juice, bourbon, almond liqueur and ice until smooth.

2. Pour into an old-fashioned glass and garnish with cherry (or cranberries).

Makes 1 serving

Tropical Canadian

Something like 80% of the world's maple syrup is produced in Canada, and on some beaches in Mexico and Cuba, especially during the winter, one might be forgiven for thinking that Canadians are the majority population of these tropical climes — so why not a "Tropical Canadian"?

¼ cup	frozen diced ripe mango	50 mL
¼ cup	apple cider or apple juice	50 mL
3 tbsp	frozen cubed pineapple	45 mL
2 tsp	grenadine	10 mL
1 tsp	pure maple syrup	5 mL
2 oz	rye whisky	50 mL
1	pineapple wedge	1

1. In blender, on high speed, blend mango, apple cider, frozen pineapple, grenadine, maple syrup and whisky until smooth.

2. Pour into an old-fashioned glass and garnish with pineapple wedge.

Makes 1 serving

Maple Leaf

1 tbsp	freshly squeezed lemon juice	15 mL
1 tbsp	pure maple syrup	15 mL
2 oz	rye whisky	50 mL
2	ice cubes	2

1. In blender, on high speed, blend lemon juice, maple syrup, whisky and ice until slushy.

2. Pour into an old-fashioned glass.

Makes 1 serving

Honey Cream

¼ cup	light (5%) cream	50 mL
2 tbsp	Honey Syrup (see page 5)	25 mL
1½ oz	bourbon	40 mL
2	ice cubes	2

1. In blender, on high speed, blend cream, Honey Syrup, bourbon and ice until smooth.

2. Pour into an old-fashioned glass.

Sometimes the simplest cocktail can be the most appealing. If you want a creamy, sweet treat, try this one. For an even richer drink, add an egg yolk (or 2 tbsp/ 25 mL pasteurized liquid whole egg, if the food safety of raw eggs is a concern for you) and sprinkle with a light pinch of freshly grated nutmeg or ground cinnamon.

Makes 1 serving

Irish 'n' Scotch Coffee

⅓ cup	chilled strong coffee or espresso	75 mL
1 oz	Scotch whisky	25 mL
1 oz	Irish cream liqueur	25 mL
2	ice cubes	2
3	chocolate-covered coffee beans	3

1. In blender, on high speed, blend coffee, Scotch, Irish cream liqueur and ice until blended.

2. Pour into an old-fashioned glass and garnish with coffee beans.

Makes 1 serving

Peach Julep

1 cup	frozen sliced peaches or nectarines	250 mL
2 tsp	chopped fresh mint	10 mL
2 oz	bourbon	50 mL
½ oz	peach schnapps	15 mL
3	ice cubes	3
1	sprig fresh mint	1

1. In blender, on high speed, blend peaches, chopped mint, bourbon, peach schnapps and ice until smooth.

2. Strain through a fine sieve into an old-fashioned glass and garnish with mint sprig.

Makes 1 serving

Minty Peach

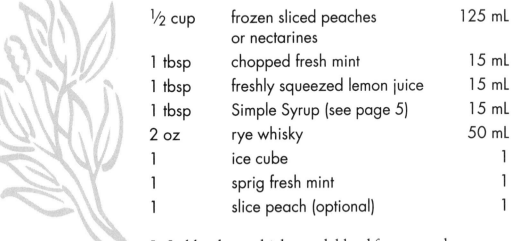

½ cup	frozen sliced peaches or nectarines	125 mL
1 tbsp	chopped fresh mint	15 mL
1 tbsp	freshly squeezed lemon juice	15 mL
1 tbsp	Simple Syrup (see page 5)	15 mL
2 oz	rye whisky	50 mL
1	ice cube	1
1	sprig fresh mint	1
1	slice peach (optional)	1

1. In blender, on high speed, blend frozen peaches, chopped mint, lemon juice, Simple Syrup, bourbon and ice until smooth.

2. Pour or strain through a fine sieve into an old-fashioned glass and garnish with mint sprig and peach slice, if desired.

Makes 1 serving

Apricot Vanilla Julep

1 cup	frozen pitted apricots or drained canned apricots	250 mL
2 tsp	chopped fresh mint	10 mL
1 ½ oz	bourbon	40 mL
½ oz	apricot brandy	15 mL
½ oz	vanilla vodka	15 mL
3	ice cubes	3
1	sprig fresh mint	1

1. In blender, on high speed, blend apricots, chopped mint, bourbon, brandy, vodka and ice until smooth.

2. Strain through a fine sieve into an old-fashioned glass and garnish with mint sprig.

Makes 1 serving

Frozen Mint Julep

3	ice cubes	3
3 tbsp	freshly squeezed lemon juice	45 mL
2 tbsp	Simple Syrup (see page 5)	25 mL
1 tbsp	chopped fresh mint	15 mL
1 ½ oz	bourbon	40 mL
1	sprig fresh mint	1

1. In blender, pulse ice until crushed. On high speed, blend in lemon juice, Simple Syrup, chopped mint and bourbon until smooth.

2. Pour into an old-fashioned glass and garnish with mint sprig.

Makes 1 serving

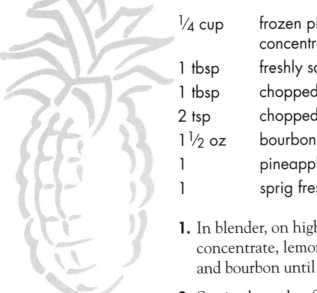

Ginger Mint Julep

1/4 cup	frozen pineapple juice concentrate	50 mL
1 tbsp	freshly squeezed lemon juice	15 mL
1 tbsp	chopped fresh mint	15 mL
2 tsp	chopped crystallized ginger	10 mL
1 1/2 oz	bourbon	40 mL
1	pineapple wedge	1
1	sprig fresh mint	1

1. In blender, on high speed, blend pineapple juice concentrate, lemon juice, chopped mint, ginger and bourbon until smooth.

2. Strain through a fine sieve into a martini or wine glass and garnish with pineapple wedge and mint sprig.

Makes 1 serving

Ginger piques the interest in a cocktail. You can substitute ginger beer for the ginger ale and crystallized ginger.

Southern Ginger

2 tbsp	freshly squeezed lemon juice	25 mL
1 tbsp	Simple Syrup (see page 5)	15 mL
1 tsp	chopped crystallized ginger	5 mL
2 oz	Tennessee whiskey	50 mL
2	ice cubes	2
1/2 cup	chilled ginger ale	125 mL
1	slice lemon	1
1	maraschino cherry	1

1. In blender, on high speed, blend lemon juice, Simple Syrup, ginger, whiskey and ice until smooth.

2. Pour into a highball glass and top with ginger ale. Garnish with lemon slice and cherry.

Makes 1 serving

Gingered Lemonade

3	ice cubes	3
¼ cup	freshly squeezed lemon juice	50 mL
2 tbsp	Simple Syrup (see page 5)	25 mL
2 tsp	chopped crystallized ginger	10 mL
1½ oz	bourbon or Tennessee whiskey	40 mL
⅓ cup	chilled ginger beer or ginger ale	75 mL
1	twist lemon rind	1

1. In blender, pulse ice until crushed. On high speed, blend in lemon juice, Simple Syrup, ginger and bourbon until slushy.

2. Pour into an old-fashioned glass and top with ginger beer. Garnish with lemon twist.

Makes 1 serving

Tennessee Lemonade

2 tbsp	freshly squeezed lemon juice	25 mL
2 tbsp	Simple Syrup (see page 5)	25 mL
1 oz	Tennessee whiskey	25 mL
1 oz	lemon vodka	25 mL
2	ice cubes	2
½ cup	chilled lemon-lime soda	125 mL
1	slice lemon or lime	1

1. In blender, on high speed, blend lemon juice, Simple Syrup, whiskey, vodka and ice until smooth.

2. Pour into a highball glass and top with lemon-lime soda. Garnish with lemon or lime slice.

Makes 1 serving

Orange Big Easy

¼ cup	freshly squeezed orange juice	50 mL
1 ½ oz	bourbon	40 mL
½ oz	orange liqueur	15 mL
3	ice cubes	3
¼ cup	chilled ginger ale	50 mL
1	slice orange	1

1. In blender, on high speed, blend orange juice, bourbon, orange liqueur and ice until smooth.

2. Pour into a highball glass and top with ginger ale. Garnish with orange slice.

Makes 1 serving

Hint o' Mint Frozen Lemon Bourbon

3	ice cubes	3
2	fresh mint leaves	2
¼ cup	frozen lemonade concentrate	50 mL
¼ cup	freshly squeezed lemon juice	50 mL
2 oz	bourbon	50 mL
1	sprig fresh mint	1

1. In blender, pulse ice, mint leaves and lemonade concentrate until ice is crushed. On high speed, blend in lemon juice and bourbon until slushy.

2. Pour into a wine or martini glass and garnish with mint sprig.

Sour Puss

The sweetness of bourbon perfectly balances the tartness of lemons.

1/4 cup	frozen lemonade concentrate	50 mL
2 oz	bourbon	50 mL
2	ice cubes	2
1	maraschino cherry	1

1. In blender, on high speed, blend lemonade concentrate, bourbon and ice until blended.

2. Pour into a martini glass and garnish with cherry.

Pucker Puss

This is a drink for lovers of tart cocktails — a real taste bud awakener.

3 tbsp	freshly squeezed lemon juice	45 mL
2 tbsp	frozen lemonade concentrate	25 mL
2 oz	bourbon	50 mL
2	ice cubes	2
1	twist lemon rind	1

1. In blender, on high speed, blend lemon juice, lemonade concentrate, bourbon and ice until blended.

2. Pour into an old-fashioned glass and garnish with lemon twist.

Makes 1 serving

Apple Orchard

¼ cup	apple cider or apple juice	50 mL
2 tbsp	frozen lemonade concentrate	25 mL
1½ oz	Tennessee whiskey	40 mL
1	ice cube	1
1	thin slice apple or slice lemon	1

1. In blender, on high speed, blend apple cider, lemonade concentrate, whiskey and ice until smooth.

2. Pour into a highball glass and garnish with apple or lemon slice.

Makes 1 serving

Berry-Berry Lemonade

You won't get beriberi if you drink enough of this vitamin-packed cocktail.

8	frozen raspberries	8
¼ cup	frozen lemonade concentrate	50 mL
¼ cup	cranberry juice	50 mL
1½ oz	bourbon	40 mL
1 oz	raspberry liqueur or framboise	25 mL
¼ cup	chilled soda water	50 mL
1	twist lemon rind	1

1. In blender, on high speed, blend raspberries, lemonade concentrate, cranberry juice, bourbon and raspberry liqueur until smooth.

2. Pour into an old-fashioned glass and top with soda. Garnish with lemon twist.

Makes 1 serving

Kentucky Lemonade

¼ cup	lemon sorbet	50 mL
¼ cup	apple cider or apple juice	50 mL
1½ oz	bourbon	40 mL
½ oz	melon liqueur	15 mL
¼ cup	chilled ginger beer	50 mL
1	slice lemon	1
1	thin slice apple	1

1. In blender, on high speed, blend sorbet, apple cider, bourbon and melon liqueur until smooth.

2. Pour into an old-fashioned glass and top with ginger beer. Garnish with lemon and apple slices.

Makes 1 serving

Blackberry Lemonade

When blackberries are in season, garnish liberally with them; otherwise, rely on frozen blackberries to make cocktails and garnish with a secondary ingredient.

6	frozen blackberries	6
¼ cup	lemon sorbet	50 mL
¼ cup	apple cider or apple juice	50 mL
1½ oz	Tennessee whiskey	40 mL
¾ oz	crème de cassis, raspberry liqueur or framboise	22 mL
¼ cup	chilled soda water	50 mL
3	fresh blackberries, skewered (optional)	3
1	slice lemon	1

1. In blender, on high speed, blend frozen blackberries, sorbet, apple cider, whiskey and crème de cassis until smooth.

2. Pour into a highball glass and top with soda. Garnish with skewered blackberries, if desired, and lemon slice.

Makes 1 serving

Iced Tea Blaster

This blender version of Long Island iced tea, like the original, is a strong drink that looks like iced tea although there's no tea in it.

¼ cup	lemon sorbet	50 mL
¾ oz	bourbon	22 mL
½ oz	citrus vodka or vodka	15 mL
½ oz	gin	15 mL
½ oz	orange liqueur	15 mL
2	ice cubes	2
¼ cup	chilled cola	50 mL
1	lemon wedge	1

1. In blender, on high speed, blend sorbet, bourbon, vodka, gin, orange liqueur and ice until smooth.

2. Pour into a highball glass and top with cola. Garnish with lemon wedge.

Makes 1 serving

Frozen Ward Eight

Ward Eight is a classic Boston cocktail first made in 1898.

¼ cup	lemon sorbet	50 mL
2 tbsp	orange juice	25 mL
½ tsp	grenadine	2 mL
2 oz	bourbon	50 mL
1	slice orange	1
1	maraschino cherry	1

1. In blender, on high speed, blend sorbet, orange juice, grenadine and bourbon until smooth.

2. Pour into a large martini glass and garnish with orange slice and cherry.

Makes 1 serving

Blazing Peach

TIP

Look for peach nectar or juice in bottles or cartons in the fruit juice section of well-stocked supermarkets and health food stores.

¼ cup	orange sorbet	50 mL
¼ cup	peach nectar or juice (see tip, at left)	50 mL
¼ cup	cranberry juice	50 mL
1 oz	bourbon	25 mL
1 oz	peach brandy	25 mL
1	maraschino cherry or slice peach	1

1. In blender, on high speed, blend sorbet, peach nectar, cranberry juice, bourbon and brandy until smooth.

2. Pour into a piña colada or old-fashioned glass and garnish with cherry or peach slice.

Makes 1 serving

Port-Whiskey Punch

¼ cup	lemon sorbet	50 mL
3 tbsp	cranberry juice	45 mL
3 tbsp	orange juice	45 mL
1½ oz	Tennessee whiskey	40 mL
1 oz	port wine	25 mL
2	ice cubes	2
1	slice orange	1

1. In blender, on high speed, blend sorbet, cranberry juice, orange juice, whiskey, port and ice until smooth.

2. Pour into a highball glass and garnish with orange slice.

Makes 1 serving

TIP

If you don't have caramel ice cream, you can substitute an equal amount of vanilla ice cream and add 2 tbsp (25 mL) caramel syrup.

Frozen Caramel Bourbon Apple

½ cup	caramel ice cream (see tip, at left)	125 mL
¼ cup	apple cider or apple juice	50 mL
2 oz	bourbon or Tennessee whiskey	50 mL
1	thin slice apple	1
Pinch	ground nutmeg	Pinch

1. In blender, on high speed, blend ice cream, apple cider and bourbon until smooth.

2. Pour into a wine or piña colada glass, garnish with apple slice and sprinkle with nutmeg.

Makes 1 serving

You can also make this with bourbon and call it a Kentucky Cream.

Jack Splat

¼ cup	caramel ice cream	50 mL
2 oz	Tennessee whiskey	50 mL
1	ice cube	1
½ tsp	liquid honey	2 mL
	Dark brown sugar, for rimming	
1 tsp	whipping (35%) cream	5 mL

1. In blender, on high speed, blend ice cream, whiskey and ice until smooth.

2. Wet the rim of an old-fashioned glass with honey and dip in brown sugar. Pour ice cream mixture into glass and drizzle with whipping cream.

Makes 1 serving

Howlin' Moon

¼ cup	vanilla ice cream	50 mL
¼ cup	pineapple juice	50 mL
2 tbsp	creamed coconut	25 mL
1 ½ oz	bourbon	40 mL
½ oz	coconut or amber rum	15 mL
1	thin round slice pineapple	1

1. In blender, on high speed, blend ice cream, pineapple juice, creamed coconut, bourbon and rum until smooth.

2. Pour into a piña colada or old-fashioned glass and garnish with pineapple slice.

Makes 1 serving

Mint Jubilee

¼ cup	vanilla ice cream	50 mL
2 oz	bourbon	50 mL
1 oz	white crème de menthe	25 mL
1	fresh mint leaf (optional)	1

1. In blender, on high speed, blend ice cream, bourbon and crème de menthe until smooth.

2. Pour into an old-fashioned glass and garnish with mint, if desired.

Makes 1 serving

You can have your cookies and drink them too with this dessert drink. If you wish, garnish with a bit of crushed amaretti.

Amaretti Cookie

3	amaretti (Italian almond cookies), crumbled	3
1/3 cup	vanilla ice cream	75 mL
Dash	almond extract	Dash
1 oz	bourbon	25 mL
1 oz	almond liqueur	25 mL

1. In blender, on high speed, blend amaretti, ice cream, almond extract, bourbon and almond liqueur until smooth.

2. Pour into an old-fashioned or wine glass.

Makes 1 serving

Irish Coffee Smoothie

1/4 cup	coffee or vanilla ice cream	50 mL
1/4 cup	chilled strong coffee or espresso	50 mL
1 oz	Irish whiskey	25 mL
1 oz	Irish cream liqueur	25 mL
1	ice cube	1

1. In blender, on high speed, blend ice cream, coffee, whiskey, Irish cream liqueur and ice until smooth.

2. Pour into an old-fashioned glass.

tequila

For over 1,000 years, Mexicans have been enjoying a type of beer called pulque, which is fermented from the mashed pulp of the blue agave plant. When the Spaniards invaded Mexico, they discovered that distilled pulque is equally palatable and, obviously, more potent — hence, tequila. White tequila is not aged, while gold tequila is aged in oak casks to give it extra smoothness and add general wood flavor attributes.

Under Mexican law, tequila must be produced in the state of Jalisco, where blue agave is native, and must be made from at least 51% blue agave mash. The more blue agave, the better, and premium brands made from 100% blue agave demand high prices. For blender cocktails, top-shelf brands of white or gold tequila will suffice — save your *añejo* (aged) high-percentage blue agave tequilas for straight shots.

Distilled mescal, made from other varieties of agave and famous for the worm often found in the bottom of the bottle, is made throughout Mexico. It has a somewhat smoky taste and can be quite rough, but finer versions are available and can be used as you would tequila.

TEQUILA RECIPES

Makes 1 serving

Frozen Margarita

The margarita is the classic tequila cocktail and has inspired countless variations.

2	ice cubes	2
1 tbsp	freshly squeezed lime juice	15 mL
2 oz	tequila	50 mL
1/2 oz	orange liqueur	1 mL
	Coarse salt, for rimming	

1. In blender, pulse ice cubes until crushed. On high speed, blend in lime juice, tequila and orange liqueur until slushy.

2. Pour into a margarita glass rimmed with salt.

Makes 1 serving

Frozen Strawberry Margarita

1	ice cube	1
10	frozen strawberries	10
2 tbsp	strawberry syrup	25 mL
1 tbsp	freshly squeezed lime juice	15 mL
2 tsp	freshly squeezed lemon juice	10 mL
2 oz	tequila	50 mL
1/2 oz	orange liqueur	15 mL
	Coarse salt, for rimming	

1. In blender, pulse ice and strawberries until ice is crushed. On high speed, blend in strawberry syrup, lime and lemon juices, tequila and orange liqueur until slushy.

2. Pour into a margarita glass rimmed with salt.

Makes 1 serving

TIP

To peel a fresh peach, submerge it in boiling water for 10 to 15 seconds to loosen the skin. Or use drained canned peaches or frozen sliced peaches.

Frozen Peach Margarita

2	ice cubes	2
½ cup	cubed peeled peaches (see tip, at left)	125 mL
2 tbsp	freshly squeezed lime juice	25 mL
½ tsp	confectioner's (icing) sugar	2 mL
1 oz	tequila	25 mL
1 oz	orange liqueur	25 mL
1 oz	peach schnapps	25 mL
	Coarse salt, for rimming	

1. In blender, pulse ice and peaches until ice is crushed. On high speed, blend in lime juice, sugar, tequila, orange liqueur and peach schnapps until slushy.

2. Pour into a margarita glass rimmed with salt.

Makes 1 serving

Raspberry Margarita

¼ cup	raspberry juice	50 mL
1 tbsp	freshly squeezed lime juice	15 mL
1 oz	tequila	25 mL
½ oz	orange liqueur	15 mL
½ oz	raspberry liqueur or framboise	15 mL
2	ice cubes	2
3	fresh raspberries (or 1 lime wedge)	3

1. In blender, on high speed, blend raspberry juice, lime juice, tequila, orange liqueur, raspberry liqueur and ice until smooth.

2. Pour into a margarita or piña colada glass and garnish with raspberries (or lime wedge).

Makes 1 serving

Mango Margarita

⅓ cup	mango nectar or juice (see tip, at left)	75 mL
¼ cup	frozen cubed ripe mango	50 mL
1 tbsp	freshly squeezed lime juice	15 mL
2 tsp	Simple Syrup (see page 5)	10 mL
1½ oz	tequila	40 mL
1 oz	orange liqueur	25 mL
	Salt, for rimming	

TIP

Look for mango nectar or juice in bottles or cartons in the fruit juice section of well-stocked supermarkets and health food stores.

1. In blender, on high speed, blend mango nectar, mango, lime juice, Simple Syrup, tequila and orange liqueur until smooth.

2. Pour into a margarita glass rimmed with salt.

Makes 1 serving

Passion Fruit Margarita

¼ cup	passion fruit nectar or juice (see tip, at left)	50 mL
1 tbsp	freshly squeezed lime juice	15 mL
1 oz	tequila	25 mL
½ oz	orange liqueur	15 mL
½ oz	passion fruit cognac	15 mL
2	ice cubes	2
1	orange or lime wedge	1

TIP

Look for passion fruit nectar or juice in bottles or cartons in the fruit juice section of well-stocked supermarkets and health food stores.

1. In blender, on high speed, blend passion fruit nectar, lime juice, tequila, orange liqueur, passion fruit cognac and ice until smooth.

2. Pour into a margarita or piña colada glass and garnish with orange or lime wedge.

Golden Blue Margarita

Blue curaçao, which is flavored with bitter orange peel from the Caribbean island of Curaçao, can give cocktails a beautiful hue, especially when combined with other ingredients.

3 tbsp	frozen limeade concentrate	45 mL
2 tbsp	orange juice	25 mL
1 ½ oz	gold tequila	40 mL
½ oz	blue curaçao	15 mL
½ oz	orange liqueur	15 mL
2	ice cubes	2
	Salt, for rimming	
1	lime wedge	1

1. In blender, on high speed, blend limeade concentrate, orange juice, tequila, blue curaçao, orange liqueur and ice until smooth.

2. Pour into a margarita glass rimmed with salt and garnish with lime wedge.

Bloody Margarita

Blood, or Moro, oranges are available during the winter and early spring months and add a festive color and intense flavor to cocktails. When they are out of season, you can substitute orange and/or tangerine juice and add a dash of grenadine for coloring.

¼ cup	freshly squeezed blood orange juice	50 mL
1 tbsp	freshly squeezed lime juice	15 mL
1 ½ oz	tequila	40 mL
½ oz	orange liqueur	15 mL
3	ice cubes	3
	Lime juice, for rimming	
	Salt, for rimming	
1	slice blood orange or lime	1

1. In blender, on high speed, blend blood orange juice, lime juice, tequila, orange liqueur and ice until smooth.

2. Pour into a margarita glass rimmed with lime juice and salt. Garnish with orange or lime slice.

Makes 1 serving

Cranberry Kiss

3 tbsp	cranberry juice	45 mL
3 tbsp	orange juice	45 mL
1 oz	tequila	25 mL
½ oz	orange liqueur	15 mL
2	ice cubes	2
3	frozen cranberries (or 1 slice orange)	3

1. In blender, on high speed, blend cranberry juice, orange juice, tequila, orange liqueur and ice until smooth.

2. Pour into a martini glass and garnish with cranberries (or orange slice).

Makes 1 serving

Two-Berry Sky

TIP

Look for strawberry nectar or juice in bottles or cartons in the fruit juice section of well-stocked supermarkets and health food stores. If not available, substitute 8 fresh or frozen strawberries.

¼ cup	strawberry nectar or juice (see tip, at left)	50 mL
2 tsp	freshly squeezed lemon juice	10 mL
1 oz	tequila	25 mL
½ oz	raspberry liqueur or framboise	15 mL
Dash	angostura bitters	Dash
2	ice cubes	2
3	fresh raspberries (optional)	3
1	fresh strawberry (optional)	1

1. In blender, on high speed, blend strawberry nectar, lemon juice, tequila, raspberry liqueur, bitters and ice until smooth.

2. Pour into a piña colada or old-fashioned glass and garnish with raspberries and/or strawberry.

Makes 1 serving

Rosy Sunrise

You might be tempted to try this drink with breakfast, but we recommend it as an aperitif, despite its name.

1	orange or tangerine, peeled and seeded	1
1 tsp	grenadine	5 mL
1 ½ oz	tequila	40 mL

1. In blender, on high speed, blend orange, grenadine and tequila until smooth.

2. Pour into an old-fashioned glass, over ice, if desired.

Makes 1 serving

Bampira on the Roof

Bampira *is Filipino for "vampire," and this drink was inspired by an old wives' tale of a vampire on the roof.*

¼ cup	pomegranate seeds (or 2 tbsp/25 mL pomegranate juice)	50 mL
2 tbsp	orange juice	25 mL
1 tbsp	freshly squeezed lime juice	15 mL
Pinch	freshly ground black pepper	Pinch
Dash	hot pepper sauce	Dash
2 oz	tequila	50 mL
	Coarse salt, for rimming	

1. In blender, on high speed, blend pomegranate seeds, orange juice, lime juice, pepper, hot pepper sauce and tequila until flesh from pomegranate separates from seed cores.

2. Strain through a fine sieve into an old-fashioned glass rimmed with salt and filled with ice.

Salty Star Surprise

Tropical star fruit, or carambola, makes a refreshing and cooling drink, especially on a hot summer day.

1	large star fruit	1
1 tbsp	freshly squeezed lime juice	15 mL
1/4 tsp	salt	1 mL
2 oz	tequila or vodka	50 mL
3	ice cubes	3

1. Cut off waxy ridge of each section of star fruit. Cut off sections, discarding core and seeds.

2. In blender, on high speed, blend star fruit, lime juice, salt, tequila and ice until slushy.

3. Pour into an old-fashioned glass.

Makes 1 serving

Bloody Maria

Bloody Marys are given a Mexican twist with the addition of tequila.

1/4 cup	tomato juice	50 mL
1/4 cup	vegetable cocktail	50 mL
2 tsp	freshly squeezed lime juice	10 mL
Dash	hot pepper sauce	Dash
Dash	Worcestershire sauce	Dash
2 oz	tequila	50 mL
3	ice cubes	3
	Celery salt, for rimming	
1	slice cucumber	1

1. In blender, on high speed, blend tomato juice, vegetable cocktail, lime juice, hot pepper sauce, Worcestershire sauce, tequila and ice until smooth.

2. Pour into an old-fashioned glass rimmed with celery salt. Garnish with cucumber slice.

Tequila Mojito

For a sweeter version of this cocktail, substitute lemon-lime soda for the soda water.

3 tbsp	frozen lemonade concentrate	45 mL
1 tbsp	chopped fresh mint	15 mL
1 tbsp	freshly squeezed lime juice	15 mL
1 1/2 oz	tequila	40 mL
2	ice cubes	2
1/4 cup	chilled soda water	50 mL
1	sprig fresh mint	1

1. In blender, on high speed, blend lemonade concentrate, chopped mint, lime juice, tequila and ice until blended.

2. Pour into a highball glass and top with soda. Garnish with mint sprig.

Apple Passion

Makes 1 serving

TIP

Look for passion fruit nectar or juice in bottles or cartons in the fruit juice section of well-stocked supermarkets and health food stores.

1/4 cup	passion fruit nectar or juice (see tip, at left)	50 mL
3 tbsp	apple cider or apple juice	45 mL
3 tbsp	frozen limeade concentrate	45 mL
1 tsp	chopped fresh mint	5 mL
2 oz	tequila	50 mL
2	ice cubes	2
1	sprig fresh mint	1
1	thin slice apple (optional)	1

1. In blender, on high speed, blend passion fruit nectar, apple cider, limeade concentrate, chopped mint, tequila and ice until smooth.

2. Pour into a piña colada or old-fashioned glass and garnish with mint sprig and apple slice, if desired.

Makes 1 serving

Arctic Sunrise

¼ cup	frozen orange juice concentrate	50 mL
2 oz	tequila	50 mL
6	ice cubes	6
1½ tsp	grenadine	7 mL
1	slice orange	1

1. In blender, on high speed, blend orange juice concentrate, tequila and ice until slushy.

2. Pour into a highball glass and top with grenadine. Garnish with orange slice.

Makes 1 serving

Golden Melon

¼ cup	frozen pineapple juice concentrate	50 mL
1 tbsp	freshly squeezed lime juice	15 mL
1½ oz	tequila	40 mL
1 oz	melon liqueur	25 mL
1	honeydew melon ball	1
1	twist lime rind	1

1. In blender, on high speed, blend pineapple juice concentrate, lime juice, tequila and melon liqueur until smooth.

2. Pour into a martini glass. Skewer melon ball and lime twist and garnish drink.

Makes 1 serving

Tequila Wallbanger

¼ cup	orange sorbet	50 mL
1 oz	tequila	25 mL
1 oz	Galliano	25 mL
1	slice orange	1

1. In blender, on high speed, blend sorbet, tequila and Galliano until smooth.

2. Pour into a large martini glass and garnish with orange slice.

Makes 1 serving

Raspberry Silk

4	frozen raspberries	4
½ cup	raspberry frozen yogurt	125 mL
1 oz	tequila	25 mL
1 oz	white crème de cacao	25 mL
1	sprig fresh mint	1

1. In blender, on high speed, blend raspberries, frozen yogurt, tequila and crème de cacao until smooth.

2. Pour into a piña colada glass and garnish with mint sprig.

sparkling wine

CHAMPAGNE, DESERVEDLY THE MOST famous of sparkling wines, was first made in the 17th century in the Champagne region of France. A monk named Dom Perignon invented the Champagne method (*méthode champenoise*), in which the carbon monoxide produced by the yeast during fermentation remains in the bottle and carbonates the wine. There are other ways to make sparkling wine, but the Champagne method produces the best bubbles. For mixed drinks, though, any quality dry sparkling wine will suffice, as the subtleties of fine Champagne will be lost in the mixing. Your best bet is one of France's many other sparkling wines, such as Crémant d'Alsace, Crémant de Limoux or Crémant de Loire; a sparkler from the Catalonian region of Spain (Cava); a German Sekt; or one of the many fine sparkling wines produced in California, Canada, Australia and other New World wineries. Sparkling wine marries particularly well with fruit flavors, and the carbonation gives a cocktail a real boost. Once you've opened a bottle, you should drink it up, so plan for company when serving sparkling cocktails.

SPARKLING WINE RECIPES

Apricot-Orange Sparkler

3 tbsp	orange sorbet	45 mL
2 tbsp	apricot nectar or juice (see tip, at left)	25 mL
1 oz	apricot brandy	25 mL
1	ice cube	1
2 oz	chilled sparkling wine	50 mL
1	twist orange rind	1

1. In blender, on high speed, blend sorbet, apricot nectar, brandy and ice until smooth.

2. Pour into a flute and top with sparkling wine. Garnish with orange twist.

Peach Sparkler

½ cup	cubed peeled peaches (see tip, at left)	125 mL
1 oz	peach schnapps	25 mL
2	ice cubes	2
2 oz	chilled sparkling wine	50 mL

1. In blender, on high speed, blend peaches, peach schnapps and ice until smooth.

2. Pour into a wine glass and top with sparkling wine.

Makes 1 serving

Peach Melba Sparkler

⅓ cup	frozen sliced peaches, chilled cubed peeled fresh peaches or chilled drained canned peaches	75 mL
¼ cup	fresh raspberries, chilled, or frozen raspberries	50 mL
2 tbsp	whipping (35%) cream	25 mL
1 tsp	confectioner's (icing) sugar	5 mL
Dash	vanilla	Dash
½ oz	orange liqueur	15 mL
2 dashes	angostura bitters	2 dashes
1	ice cube	1
3 oz	sparkling wine	75 mL

1. In blender, on high speed, blend peaches, raspberries, whipping cream, sugar, vanilla, orange liqueur, bitters and ice until smooth.

2. Strain through a fine sieve into a large wine glass and top with sparkling wine.

Makes 1 serving

Blueberry Sparkler

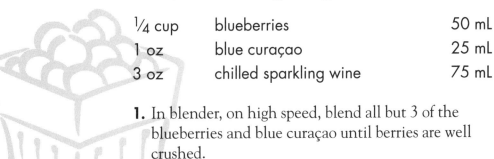

¼ cup	blueberries	50 mL
1 oz	blue curaçao	25 mL
3 oz	chilled sparkling wine	75 mL

1. In blender, on high speed, blend all but 3 of the blueberries and blue curaçao until berries are well crushed.

2. Strain through a fine sieve into a flute and top with sparkling wine. Garnish with reserved berries.

Makes 1 serving

Raspberry-Peach Sparkler

⅓ cup	cubed peeled peaches (see tip, page 176)	75 mL
⅓ cup	fresh or frozen raspberries	75 mL
1 oz	peach schnapps	25 mL
6	ice cubes	6
2 oz	chilled sparkling wine	50 mL

1. In blender, on high speed, blend peaches, raspberries, peach schnapps and ice until slushy.

2. Pour into a large wine glass and top with sparkling wine.

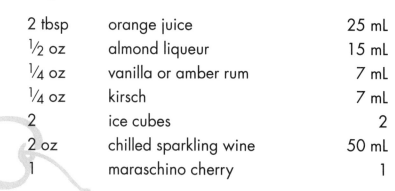

Makes 1 serving

Cherry-Almond Sparkler

2 tbsp	orange juice	25 mL
½ oz	almond liqueur	15 mL
¼ oz	vanilla or amber rum	7 mL
¼ oz	kirsch	7 mL
2	ice cubes	2
2 oz	chilled sparkling wine	50 mL
1	maraschino cherry	1

1. In blender, on high speed, blend orange juice, almond liqueur, rum, kirsch and ice until smooth.

2. Pour into a flute and top with sparkling wine. Garnish with cherry.

Pick-Me-Up Sparkler

Makes 1 serving

This fanciful variation on a classic Champagne cocktail is guaranteed to perk up the dead. Enjoy it for brunch.

1 tbsp	freshly squeezed lemon juice	15 mL
2 tsp	grenadine	10 mL
2 tsp	Simple Syrup (see page 5)	10 mL
2 oz	brandy	50 mL
2	ice cubes	2
2 oz	chilled sparkling wine	50 mL

1. In blender, on high speed, blend lemon juice, grenadine, Simple Syrup, brandy and ice until smooth.

2. Pour into a flute and top with sparkling wine.

Grapefruit Sparkler

Makes 1 serving

You can use white grapefruit juice for this sparkler, but add a dash of grenadine for an attractive hue.

½ cup	pink grapefruit juice	125 mL
1 oz	orange liqueur	25 mL
2	ice cubes	2
2 oz	chilled sparkling wine	50 mL
1	twist orange rind	1

1. In blender, on high speed, blend grapefruit juice, orange liqueur and ice until smooth.

2. Pour into a flute and top with sparkling wine. Garnish with orange twist.

Makes 1 serving

This sophisticated cocktail has a subtle blend of flavors.

TIP

Look for pear nectar or juice in bottles or cartons in the fruit juice section of well-stocked supermarkets and health food stores.

Vanilla-Pear Sparkler

¼ cup	pear nectar or juice (see tip, at left)	50 mL
1 oz	vanilla vodka	25 mL
2	ice cubes	2
2 oz	chilled sparkling wine	50 mL
1	thin slice pear	1

1. In blender, on high speed, blend pear nectar, vodka and ice until smooth.

2. Pour into a flute and top with sparkling wine. Garnish with pear slice.

Makes 1 serving

Mango Sparkler

½ cup	cubed peeled mango	125 mL
2 tbsp	orange juice	25 mL
½ oz	brandy	15 mL
2	ice cubes	2
2 oz	chilled sparkling wine	50 mL

1. In blender, on high speed, blend mango, orange juice, brandy and ice until smooth.

2. Pour into a wine glass and top with sparkling wine.

Makes 1 serving

TIP

Look for mango nectar or juice in bottles or cartons in the fruit juice section of well-stocked supermarkets and health food stores.

Mango Margarita Sparkler

3 tbsp	mango nectar or juice (see tip, at left)	45 mL
1 tbsp	freshly squeezed lime juice	15 mL
1 oz	tequila	25 mL
1 oz	orange liqueur	25 mL
2	ice cubes	2
2 oz	chilled sparkling wine	50 mL

1. In blender, on high speed, blend mango nectar, lime juice, tequila, orange liqueur and ice until smooth.

2. Pour into a flute and top with sparkling wine.

Makes 1 serving

Pineapple Sparkler

½ cup	cubed pineapple	125 mL
1 tbsp	freshly squeezed lime juice	15 mL
½ oz	amber rum	15 mL
2	ice cubes	2
3 oz	chilled sparkling wine	75 mL

1. In blender, on high speed, blend pineapple, lime juice, rum and ice until smooth.

2. Pour into a large wine glass and top with sparkling wine.

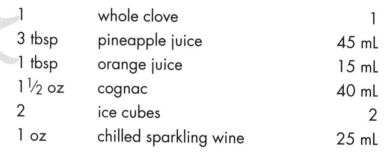

Makes 1 serving

Garnish this cocktail with a pineapple wedge studded with a whole clove, if desired.

Pineapple Clove Sparkler

1	whole clove	1
3 tbsp	pineapple juice	45 mL
1 tbsp	orange juice	15 mL
1 1/2 oz	cognac	40 mL
2	ice cubes	2
1 oz	chilled sparkling wine	25 mL

1. In blender, on high speed, blend clove, pineapple juice, orange juice, cognac and ice until smooth.

2. Strain through a fine sieve into an old-fashioned or highball glass and top with sparkling wine.

Makes 1 serving

Persimmon Sparkler

1/2 cup	cubed peeled very ripe persimmon	125 mL
2 tbsp	orange juice	25 mL
1/2 oz	brandy	15 mL
2	ice cubes	2
2 oz	chilled sparkling wine	50 mL

1. In blender, on high speed, blend persimmon, orange juice, brandy and ice until smooth.

2. Pour into a wine glass and top with sparkling wine.

Passionate Sparkler

Makes 1 serving

For a fancy garnish for this delicately hued drink, place a cape gooseberry on the rim of the flute.

TIP

Look for peach nectar or juice in bottles or cartons in the fruit juice section of well-stocked supermarkets and health food stores.

3 tbsp	peach nectar or juice (see tip, at left)	45 mL
1 tbsp	pineapple juice	15 mL
1 oz	passion fruit cognac	25 mL
2	ice cubes	2
1½ oz	chilled sparkling wine	40 mL

1. In blender, on high speed, blend peach nectar, pineapple juice, cognac and ice until smooth.

2. Pour into a flute and top with sparkling wine.

Sparkling Mojito

Makes 1 serving

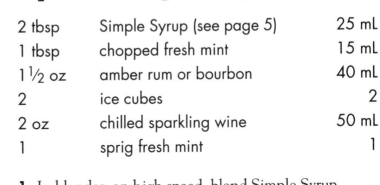

2 tbsp	Simple Syrup (see page 5)	25 mL
1 tbsp	chopped fresh mint	15 mL
1½ oz	amber rum or bourbon	40 mL
2	ice cubes	2
2 oz	chilled sparkling wine	50 mL
1	sprig fresh mint	1

1. In blender, on high speed, blend Simple Syrup, chopped mint, rum and ice until smooth.

2. Pour into a flute and top with sparkling wine. Garnish with mint sprig.

Makes 1 serving

Poinsettia

2 tbsp	frozen cranberry concentrate	25 mL
½ oz	cranberry vodka or vodka	15 mL
½ oz	orange liqueur	15 mL
2 oz	chilled sparkling wine	50 mL
1 or 2	frozen cranberries	1 or 2

1. In blender, on high speed, blend cranberry concentrate, vodka and orange liqueur until smooth.

2. Pour into a flute and top with sparkling wine. Garnish with cranberries.

Makes 1 serving

Prince of Wales

This lovely pink-blushed cocktail is perfect for Valentine's Day. You can also serve it in a sugar-rimmed martini glass.

1	frozen strawberry	1
1 tbsp	freshly squeezed lemon juice	15 mL
2 tsp	Simple Syrup (see page 5)	10 mL
½ oz	cherry brandy	15 mL
2	ice cubes	2
2 oz	chilled sparkling wine	50 mL
1	fresh strawberry or maraschino cherry	1

1. In blender, on high speed, blend frozen strawberry, lemon juice, Simple Syrup, brandy and ice until slushy.

2. Pour into a flute and top with sparkling wine. Garnish with strawberry or cherry.

Makes 1 serving

Summer Melon

¼ cup	lemon sorbet	50 mL
¼ cup	cubed ripe cantaloupe	50 mL
¼ cup	cubed ripe honeydew melon	50 mL
1 oz	melon liqueur	25 mL
2 oz	chilled pink sparkling wine or sparkling wine	50 mL
3	cantaloupe balls, skewered	3

1. In blender, on high speed, blend sorbet, cantaloupe, honeydew melon and melon liqueur until smooth.

2. Pour into a piña colada glass and top with sparkling wine. Garnish with skewered cantaloupe balls.

Makes 1 serving

TIP

To peel a fresh peach, submerge it in boiling water for 10 to 15 seconds to loosen the skin. Or use drained canned peaches or frozen sliced peaches.

Blender Bellini

2	ice cubes	2
½ cup	cubed peeled peaches (see tip, at left)	125 mL
2 tsp	freshly squeezed lemon juice	10 mL
1 tsp	grenadine	5 mL
½ oz	peach schnapps	15 mL
2 oz	chilled sparkling wine	50 mL

1. In blender, pulse ice and peach until ice is crushed. On high speed, blend in lemon juice, grenadine and peach schnapps until slushy.

2. Pour into a wide-mouthed champagne glass or a martini glass and top with sparkling wine.

Bellinitini

Makes 1 serving

TIP

Look for peach nectar or juice in bottles or cartons in the fruit juice section of well-stocked supermarkets and health food stores.

2 tbsp	peach nectar or juice (see tip, at left)	25 mL
1 oz	vodka	25 mL
½ oz	crème de cassis	15 mL
½ oz	peach schnapps	15 mL
2	ice cubes	2
2 oz	chilled sparkling wine	50 mL
1	slice fresh peach (or 3 fresh black currants) (optional)	1

1. In blender, on high speed, blend peach nectar, vodka, crème de cassis, peach schnapps and ice until smooth.

2. Pour into a flute and top with sparkling wine. Garnish with peach slice (or black currants), if desired.

Makes 1 serving

Orange Fizz

¼ cup	freshly squeezed orange juice	50 mL
1 oz	amber or white rum	25 mL
2	ice cubes	2
2 oz	chilled sparkling wine	50 mL
1	twist orange rind	1

1. In blender, on high speed, blend orange juice, rum and ice until smooth.

2. Pour into a flute and top with sparkling wine. Garnish with orange twist.

Makes 1 serving

Black Currant Orange Royale

2 tbsp	orange juice	25 mL
1 oz	crème de cassis	25 mL
2	ice cubes	2
2 oz	chilled sparkling wine	50 mL
1	twist orange rind	1

1. In blender, on high speed, blend orange juice, crème de cassis and ice until smooth.

2. Pour into a flute and top with sparkling wine. Garnish with orange twist.

Makes 1 serving

TIP

Look for pomegranate-cherry juice in bottles or cartons in the fruit juice section of well-stocked supermarkets and health food stores. If you can't find it, you can use freshly squeezed pomegranate juice. To juice a pomegranate, cut it in half and use a citrus reamer or juicer; strain. One large pomegranate will yield about ½ cup (125 mL) juice.

Pomegranate-Cherry Royale

2 tbsp	pomegranate-cherry juice or pomegranate juice (see tip, at left)	25 mL
½ oz	crème de cassis	15 mL
½ oz	cherry brandy	15 mL
2	ice cubes	2
2 oz	chilled sparkling wine	50 mL
1	fresh cherry (optional)	1

1. In blender, on high speed, blend pomegranate-cherry juice, crème de cassis, brandy and ice until smooth.

2. Pour into a flute and top with sparkling wine. Garnish with cherry, if desired.

sake

ALTHOUGH IT IS KNOWN as Japanese rice wine, sake is actually fermented like a beer from rice, both non-glutinous and glutinous varieties. Sake has only recently been introduced to the cocktail repertoire, but its popularity is soaring in North America. Japanese drinkers have experimented with drinking sake on the rocks and with adding various flavoring agents, such as lemon or sour plums, but they usually drink it straight, cold, at room temperature or warmed, with meals.

Most Asian countries produce rice "wines," but Japanese sake is singular in its relatively light and clean palate, making it eminently more suitable to blended cocktails than other rice wines. Most sake has a hint of sweetness, particularly sake made from sweeter glutinous rice. There are filtered and unfiltered sakes (sometimes called "cream sakes"), the latter being slightly cloudy and with some residue of the rice lees at the bottom of the bottle. Clear, filtered sake is obviously the best for clear cocktails, but if you are mixing sake with fruit, for instance, you might like to experiment with the full-flavored unfiltered sake.

SAKE RECIPES

Makes 1 serving

Apple Saketini

Mellow sake pairs surprisingly well with all kinds of fruit.

¼ cup	apple juice	50 mL
1 oz	sake	25 mL
1 oz	vodka or apple vodka	25 mL
1	ice cube	1
1	thin slice apple	1

1. In blender, on high speed, blend apple juice, sake, vodka and ice until smooth.

2. Pour into a martini glass and garnish with apple slice.

Makes 1 serving

TIP

Look for peach nectar or juice in bottles or cartons in the fruit juice section of well-stocked supermarkets and health food stores.

Peach Saketini

3 tbsp	peach nectar or juice (see tip, at left)	45 mL
1½ oz	sake	40 mL
1½ oz	passion fruit liqueur	40 mL
2	ice cubes	2
1	thin slice fresh peach (optional)	1

1. In blender, on high speed, blend peach nectar, sake, passion fruit liqueur and ice until smooth.

2. Pour into a martini glass and garnish with peach slice, if desired.

Ruby Red Saketini

3 tbsp	blood orange or orange juice	45 mL
2 tbsp	cranberry juice	25 mL
1 oz	sake	25 mL
1 oz	vodka	25 mL
2	ice cubes	2
1	twist orange rind	1

1. In blender, on high speed, blend orange juice, cranberry juice, sake, vodka and ice until smooth.

2. Pour into a martini glass and garnish with orange twist.

Melon Saketini

Sake and gin combine to add an intriguing flavor to this melon cocktail.

¼ cup	frozen cubed ripe honeydew melon	50 mL
2 oz	sake	50 mL
1 oz	gin	25 mL
½ oz	melon liqueur	15 mL
1	honeydew melon ball	1

1. In blender, on high speed, blend honeydew melon, sake, gin and melon liqueur until smooth.

2. Pour into a martini glass and garnish with melon ball.

Makes 1 serving

Kiwitini

⅓ cup	frozen chopped peeled kiwi fruit	75 mL
1 oz	sake	25 mL
1 oz	vodka	25 mL
½ oz	melon liqueur	15 mL
2	ice cubes	2
1	slice kiwi fruit	1

1. In blender, on high speed, blend frozen kiwi, sake, vodka, melon liqueur and ice until smooth.

2. Pour into a large martini glass and garnish with kiwi slice.

Makes 1 serving

TIP

Look for passion fruit nectar or juice in bottles or cartons in the fruit juice section of well-stocked supermarkets and health food stores.

Passiontini

¼ cup	passion fruit nectar or juice (see tip, at left)	50 mL
1 oz	sake	25 mL
1 oz	vodka or orange vodka	25 mL
½ oz	passion fruit liqueur	15 mL
2	ice cubes	2
1	slice orange	1

1. In blender, on high speed, blend passion fruit nectar, sake, vodka, passion fruit liqueur and ice until smooth.

2. Pour into a large martini or wine glass and garnish with orange slice.

Blood Orange Slushy (page 203)

Overleaf: Irish Cream Coffee (page 223)

Lichee-Pear Saketini

This modern fusion drink is pretty darn delicious!

TIP

Look for pear nectar or juice in bottles or cartons in the fruit juice section of well-stocked supermarkets and health food stores.

3 tbsp	pear nectar or juice (see tip, at left)	45 mL
1 ½ oz	sake	40 mL
1 ½ oz	lichee liqueur	40 mL
2	ice cubes	2
1	fresh or drained canned lichee or thin slice Asian pear	1

1. In blender, on high speed, blend pear nectar, sake, lichee liqueur and ice until smooth.

2. Pour into a martini glass and garnish with lichee or pear slice.

Asian Pear Saketini

¼ cup	cubed peeled very ripe Asian pear or pear	50 mL
1 oz	sake	25 mL
1 oz	vodka or citrus vodka	25 mL
2	ice cubes	2
1	twist lemon rind	1

1. In blender, on high speed, blend pear, sake, vodka and ice until smooth.

2. Pour into a martini glass and garnish with lemon twist.

Overleaf: Little Miss Pink (page 227)

Sangria for Beginners (page 234)

Makes 1 serving

Cucumber Saketini

The flavors of cucumber and sake are remarkably well-suited to each other, and a touch of rose adds another layer to the delicate bouquet.

3 tbsp	diced cored peeled English cucumber	45 mL
Dash	rosewater (optional)	Dash
1 oz	sake	25 mL
1 oz	vodka	25 mL
2	ice cubes	2
1	thin slice cucumber or unsprayed rose petal	1

1. In blender, on high speed, blend diced cucumber, rosewater (if using), sake, vodka and ice until smooth.

2. Strain through a fine sieve into a martini glass and garnish with cucumber slice or rose petal.

Makes 1 serving

Cuc'a Sake Martini

¼ cup	chopped seeded peeled cucumber	50 mL
1 tsp	freshly squeezed lemon juice	5 mL
3 oz	sake	75 mL
1	ice cube	1
	Twist of cucumber peel	

1. In blender, on high speed, blend cucumber, lemon juice, sake and ice until smooth.

2. Pour into a martini glass and garnish with cucumber peel.

Makes 1 serving

Melon Madness

2 tsp	freshly squeezed lime juice	10 mL
1 oz	sake	25 mL
1 oz	melon liqueur	25 mL
2	ice cubes	2
1	honeydew melon ball	1

1. In blender, on high speed, blend lime juice, sake, melon liqueur and ice until smooth.

2. Pour into a martini glass and garnish with melon ball.

Makes 1 serving

Melon Sakequiri

This pretty light green cocktail can be served in half-portions as an entre-cours (refreshment between courses) at the dinner table.

½ cup	cubed ripe honeydew melon	125 mL
¼ cup	lime sorbet	50 mL
2 oz	sake	50 mL
1	slice lime	1

1. In blender, on high speed, blend honeydew melon, sorbet and sake until smooth.

2. Pour into a piña colada glass and garnish with lime slice.

liqueurs, aperitifs
and more

LIQUEURS ARE AN ESSENTIAL ingredient in the repertoire of blender drinks. Liqueurs and aperitifs (sometimes called cordials in North America) are made from sweetened distilled spirits to which fruits, herbs, florals and/or spices have been added for flavoring. Most liqueurs use fairly neutral grain spirits, while aperitifs are usually made with distillations from wine, such as brandy, marc or grappa. Eaux de vie (literally "waters of life") are usually distilled directly from fruit mashes and are not commonly sweetened. Fortified wines are wines to which spirits have been added to boost the alcohol content and avoid spoilage. They are usually dense with flavor and have varying degrees of sweetness.

Liqueurs are useful for our purposes because they harbor the essential flavors of fruits and other ingredients essential to a good cocktail. Raspberry, orange, coffee, hazelnut and almond liqueurs come up time and again in our recipes to add just the right touch to our cocktails, as do crème liqueurs, such as mint (crème de menthe) and banana (crème de banane). Aperitifs, such as Campari or vermouth, are used less often, but when they are, they add the perfect amount of herbal taste or bitterness to a drink. Any good bar must stock a large variety of liqueurs; luckily, their added sugar helps prolong their shelf life.

Eaux de vie are often very expensive, as good ones must be made with hand-picked fruit at the absolute height of ripeness and the mash must begin distillation within hours. Being high in alcohol content, however, they have long shelf lives. We use them sparingly, but they are also essential. Kirsch (cherry eau de vie) is a traditional partner to cherry and almond desserts, and its function in cocktails is similar. Poire William (pear eau de vie) tastes like a heavenly essence of pear and can be used in small amounts to highlight pear flavors in drinks.

Fortified wines, such as Italian Marsala, Spanish sherry, Portuguese Madeira and port, and French Lillet, are most often appreciated on their own, but their occasional use in cocktails highlights their individual flavors. Once opened, most will lose their flavor within weeks, so its best to buy small bottles and enjoy them quickly, both in cocktails and as they are.

LIQUEURS, APERITIFS AND MORE: RECIPES

Makes 1 serving

When you pair fresh fruit with eau de vie of the same flavor, the resulting drink evokes the essence of the fruit.

Essence of Pear Martini

¼ cup	cubed peeled very ripe pear	50 mL
1½ oz	pear eau de vie (Poire William)	40 mL
1	ice cube	1

1. In blender, on high speed, blend pear, pear eau de vie and ice until smooth.

2. Pour into a martini glass.

Makes 1 serving

Essence of Plum Martini

1	red or prune plum or pluot, peeled, halved and pitted	1
1½ oz	plum eau de vie (such as slivovitz or pruneaux or pflümli)	40 mL
1	ice cube	1

1. In blender, on high speed, blend plum, plum eau de vie and ice until smooth.

2. Pour into a martini glass.

Makes 1 serving

Essence of Cherry Martini

¼ cup	pitted sweet cherries	50 mL
1½ oz	cherry eau de vie (kirsch)	40 mL
1	ice cube	1

1. In blender, on high speed, blend cherries, kirsch and ice until smooth.

2. Pour into a martini glass.

Makes 1 serving

Use sweet sherry for this dessert drink if you desire a sweet cocktail.

Trifletini

10	fresh or frozen strawberries	10
¼ cup	whipping (35%) cream	50 mL
1 oz	hazelnut or almond liqueur	25 mL
1 oz	dry or sweet sherry	25 mL
1 oz	vodka	25 mL
	Ladyfingers (optional)	

1. In blender, on high speed, blend strawberries, whipping cream, hazelnut liqueur, sherry and vodka until smooth.

2. Pour into a martini glass. Serve with ladyfingers, if desired.

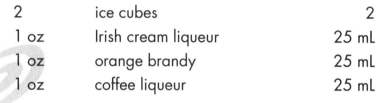

Makes 1 serving

Frozen B-52

2	ice cubes	2
1 oz	Irish cream liqueur	25 mL
1 oz	orange brandy	25 mL
1 oz	coffee liqueur	25 mL

1. In blender, pulse ice until crushed. On high speed, blend in Irish cream liqueur, orange brandy and coffee liqueur until slushy.

2. Pour into an old-fashioned glass.

Makes 1 serving

Almond Bananamania

½	frozen ripe banana	½
2 tbsp	freshly squeezed orange juice	25 mL
2 tbsp	pineapple juice	25 mL
1 oz	almond liqueur	25 mL
1 oz	crème de banane	25 mL
1	slice orange	1
1	maraschino cherry	1

1. In blender, on high speed, blend frozen banana, orange juice, pineapple juice, almond liqueur and crème de banane until smooth.

2. Pour into a piña colada glass and garnish with orange slice and cherry.

Makes 1 serving

La Vie en Rose

1 tbsp	freshly squeezed lemon juice	15 mL
1 tbsp	grenadine	15 mL
1 oz	vodka or gin	25 mL
1 oz	kirsch	25 mL
2	ice cubes	2
1	unsprayed rose petal (optional)	1

1. In blender, on high speed, blend lemon juice, grenadine, vodka, kirsch and ice until ice is well crushed.

2. Pour into an old-fashioned glass and garnish with rose petal, if desired.

Makes 1 serving

Serve this drink in a chilled martini glass in place of dessert.

Raspberry Freezie

¼ cup	raspberry sorbet	50 mL
2 oz	chilled framboise	50 mL
2 tsp	grated bittersweet chocolate	10 mL
	Fresh raspberries, for garnish	

1. In blender, on high speed, blend sorbet and framboise until smooth.

2. Pour into a martini glass, sprinkle with chocolate and garnish with raspberries.

Sapphire Fizz

This recipe contains a raw egg white. If the food safety of raw eggs is a concern for you, use the pasteurized liquid egg white instead.

1	egg white (or 2 tbsp/25 mL pasteurized liquid egg white)	1
2 tbsp	freshly squeezed lemon juice	25 mL
1 tsp	confectioner's (icing) sugar	5 mL
2 oz	blue curaçao	50 mL
1 oz	gin	25 mL
2	ice cubes	2
3 tbsp	tonic water or soda water	45 mL
1	slice lemon	1

1. In blender, on high speed, blend egg white, lemon juice, sugar, blue curaçao, gin and ice until smooth.

2. Pour into a highball glass and top with tonic water. Garnish with lemon slice.

Blue Lagoon

2 tbsp	freshly squeezed lime juice	25 mL
2 tbsp	Simple Syrup (see page 5)	25 mL
1 oz	blue curaçao	25 mL
1 oz	gin	25 mL
1 oz	vodka	25 mL
2	ice cubes	2

1. In blender, on high speed, blend lime juice, Simple Syrup, blue curaçao, gin, vodka and ice until ice is well crushed.

2. Pour into an old-fashioned glass.

Makes 1 serving

TIP

If blood oranges are out of season, use regular orange juice or orange-tangerine juice and add 2 tsp (10 mL) grenadine.

Blood Orange Slushy

½ cup	freshly squeezed blood orange juice (see tip, at left)	125 mL
2 oz	Campari	50 mL
3	ice cubes	3
1	slice blood orange or twist orange rind	1

1. In blender, on high speed, blend orange juice, Campari and ice until slushy.

2. Pour into an old-fashioned glass and garnish with orange slice or twist.

Makes 1 serving

Grapefruit Slushy

½ cup	pink or white grapefruit juice	125 mL
2 oz	Campari	50 mL
3	ice cubes	3
1	slice orange or twist orange rind	1

1. In blender, on high speed, blend grapefruit juice, Campari and ice until slushy.

2. Pour into an old-fashioned glass and garnish with orange slice or twist.

Makes 1 serving

Ruby Red Fizz

2 oz	Campari	50 mL
½ oz	orange liqueur	15 mL
2	ice cubes	2
⅓ cup	chilled orange-flavored mineral water	75 mL
1	slice orange	1

1. In blender, on high speed, blend Campari, orange liqueur and ice until smooth.

2. Pour into a highball glass and top with mineral water. Garnish with orange slice.

Makes 1 serving

Mock Gewürztraminer

This aperitif cocktail combines the lichee, rose and spice characteristics of Gewürztraminer wine. You can buy rosewater at gourmet shops and Middle Eastern grocery stores.

4	canned lichees, drained	4
1 tbsp	syrup from canned lichees	15 mL
Dash	rosewater	Dash
Dash	freshly squeezed lemon juice	Dash
3 oz	dry white vermouth	75 mL
2	ice cubes	2

1. In blender, on high speed, blend lichees, syrup, rosewater, lemon juice, vermouth and ice cubes until smooth.

2. Pour into a wine glass.

Guinness Punch

Makes 1 serving

This famous Jamaican drink blends sweet milk with bitter stout for a drink that tastes a little like a Chai milkshake.

¼ cup	sweetened condensed milk	50 mL
Pinch	ground nutmeg	Pinch
Pinch	ground cinnamon	Pinch
Pinch	unsweetened cocoa powder (optional)	Pinch
1 cup	stout (such as Guinness)	250 mL

1. In blender, on high speed, blend condensed milk, nutmeg, cinnamon, cocoa (if using) and stout until smooth and well combined.

2. Pour into a chilled beer mug or glass.

Coffee Toffee

Makes 1 serving

¼ cup	chilled strong coffee or espresso	50 mL
1½ oz	toffee cream liqueur	40 mL
½ oz	coffee liqueur	15 mL
2	ice cubes	2
3	chocolate-covered coffee beans	3

1. In blender, on high speed, blend coffee, toffee liqueur, coffee liqueur and ice until smooth.

2. Pour into an old-fashioned glass and garnish with coffee beans.

Makes 1 serving

Cinnamon Choco-Coffee

¼ cup	chilled strong coffee or espresso	50 mL
2 tbsp	chocolate syrup	25 mL
1 ½ oz	Irish cream liqueur	40 mL
½ oz	cinnamon schnapps	15 mL
2	ice cubes	2
1	cinnamon stick	1

1. In blender, on high speed, blend coffee, chocolate syrup, Irish cream liqueur, cinnamon schnapps and ice until smooth.

2. Pour into an old-fashioned glass and garnish with cinnamon stick.

Makes 1 serving

Crème de Fruits

Serve this mélange de fruits cocktail topped with a dollop of whipped cream and garnished with a few fresh blueberries and thin slices of fresh strawberry.

4	frozen strawberries	4
¼ cup	light (5%) cream	50 mL
3 tbsp	frozen blueberries	45 mL
1 oz	raspberry liqueur or framboise	25 mL
½ oz	orange liqueur	15 mL
½ oz	hazelnut liqueur	15 mL
2	ice cubes	2

1. In blender, on high speed, blend strawberries, cream, blueberries, raspberry liqueur, orange liqueur, hazelnut liqueur and ice until smooth.

2. Strain through a fine sieve into an old-fashioned glass.

Makes 1 serving

Nuts 'n' Cream

2 oz	light (5%) cream	50 mL
1 oz	hazelnut liqueur	25 mL
1 oz	Irish cream liqueur	25 mL
2	ice cubes	2

1. In blender, on high speed, blend cream, hazelnut liqueur, Irish cream liqueur and ice until smooth.

2. Pour into a large martini or wine glass.

Makes 1 serving

White Licorice

3 tbsp	light (5%) cream	45 mL
1 oz	white crème de cacao	25 mL
½ oz	white crème de menthe	15 mL
½ oz	anise liqueur, such as Pernod, ouzo or anisette	15 mL
2	ice cubes	2
1	maraschino cherry (optional)	1

1. In blender, on high speed, blend cream, crème de cacao, crème de menthe, anise liqueur and ice until smooth.

2. Pour into a martini glass and garnish with cherry, if desired.

Chocolate Bar Cocktail

½ cup	milk	125 mL
½ cup	coconut milk	125 mL
2 oz	chocolate liqueur	50 mL
½ oz	hazelnut liqueur	15 mL
4	ice cubes	4
2 tsp	grated bittersweet chocolate	10 mL

1. In blender, on high speed, blend milk, coconut milk, chocolate and hazelnut liqueurs and ice until smooth.

2. Pour into an old-fashioned glass and sprinkle with chocolate.

Summer Pimm's Slushy

¼ cup	chopped peeled seeded cucumber	50 mL
2 tsp	freshly squeezed lemon juice	10 mL
2 oz	Pimm's No. 1 liqueur	50 mL
2	ice cubes	2
¼ cup	soda water or seltzer	50 mL
1	slice lemon	1

1. In blender, on high speed, blend cucumber, lemon juice, Pimm's and ice until slushy but not altogether smooth.

2. Pour into a highball glass and top with soda. Garnish with lemon slice.

Makes 1 serving

Freezing Navel

$\frac{1}{4}$ cup	frozen orange juice concentrate	50 mL
2 oz	peach schnapps	50 mL
6	ice cubes	6
1	slice peach or orange	1

1. In blender, on high speed, blend orange juice concentrate, peach schnapps and ice until slushy.

2. Pour into a highball glass and garnish with peach slice.

Makes 1 serving

Tropical Monkey

$\frac{1}{2}$	frozen ripe banana	$\frac{1}{2}$
2 tbsp	frozen orange juice concentrate	25 mL
1 tsp	grenadine	5 mL
1 oz	crème de banane	25 mL
$\frac{1}{2}$ oz	almond liqueur	15 mL
$\frac{1}{2}$ oz	orange liqueur	15 mL
1	slice banana	1
1	maraschino cherry	1

1. In blender, on high speed, blend frozen banana, orange juice concentrate, grenadine, crème de banane, almond liqueur and orange liqueur until smooth.

2. Pour into a piña colada or wine glass and garnish with banana slice and cherry.

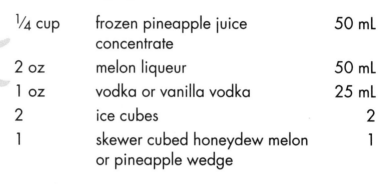

Makes 1 serving

Pineapple-Melonball

¼ cup	frozen pineapple juice concentrate	50 mL
2 oz	melon liqueur	50 mL
1 oz	vodka or vanilla vodka	25 mL
2	ice cubes	2
1	skewer cubed honeydew melon or pineapple wedge	1

1. In blender, on high speed, blend pineapple juice concentrate, melon liqueur, vodka and ice until smooth.

2. Pour into a martini or wine glass and garnish with skewered melon or pineapple wedge.

Makes 1 serving

Orange Toffee

3 tbsp	orange sorbet	45 mL
2 oz	toffee cream liqueur	50 mL
1	ice cube	1
1	twist orange rind	1

1. In blender, on high speed, blend sorbet, toffee liqueur and ice until smooth.

2. Pour into a martini glass and garnish with orange twist.

Makes 1 serving

Ruby Almond

¼ cup	orange sorbet	50 mL
1 oz	Campari	25 mL
1 oz	almond liqueur	25 mL
1	twist orange rind	1

Variation

For a less sweet version of this beautifully hued drink, replace the sorbet with 2 tbsp (25 mL) frozen orange juice concentrate and 2 ice cubes.

1. In blender, on high speed, blend sorbet, Campari and almond liqueur until smooth.

2. Pour into an old-fashioned glass and garnish with orange twist.

Makes 1 serving

Frosted Orange

¼ cup	orange frozen yogurt or ice cream	50 mL
½ oz	almond liqueur	15 mL
½ oz	hazelnut liqueur	15 mL
½ oz	orange liqueur	15 mL
1	slice orange	1
1	maraschino cherry	1

1. In blender, on high speed, blend frozen yogurt, almond liqueur, hazelnut liqueur and orange liqueur until smooth.

2. Pour into a piña colada or old-fashioned glass and garnish with orange slice and cherry.

Makes 1 serving

Frosted Raspberry

¼ cup	raspberry frozen yogurt or sorbet	50 mL
½ oz	almond liqueur	15 mL
½ oz	hazelnut liqueur	15 mL
½ oz	raspberry liqueur	15 mL
3	fresh raspberries	3

1. In blender, on high speed, blend frozen yogurt, almond liqueur, hazelnut liqueur and raspberry liqueur until smooth.

2. Pour into a piña colada or old-fashioned glass and garnish with raspberries.

Makes 1 serving

You can top this tutti-frutti drink, and the variation that follows, with any or all of these garnishes: maraschino cherry, raspberries, banana slice or orange slice.

Variation

Creamy Fruit Salad: Replace the frozen yogurt with an equal amount of vanilla ice cream.

Fruit Salad

¼ cup	orange or raspberry frozen yogurt or sorbet	50 mL
½ oz	orange liqueur	15 mL
½ oz	raspberry liqueur	15 mL
½ oz	crème de banane	15 mL

1. In blender, on high speed, blend frozen yogurt, orange liqueur, raspberry liqueur and crème de banane until smooth.

2. Pour into a piña colada or old-fashioned glass.

Makes 1 serving

Avalanche

½	frozen ripe banana	½
¼ cup	vanilla ice cream	50 mL
1 oz	crème de banane	25 mL
½ oz	white crème de cacao	15 mL
½ oz	almond liqueur	15 mL
1	slice banana	1

1. In blender, on high speed, blend frozen banana, ice cream, crème de banane, crème de cacao and almond liqueur until smooth.

2. Pour into a highball glass and garnish with banana slice.

Makes 1 serving

Pink Banana Split

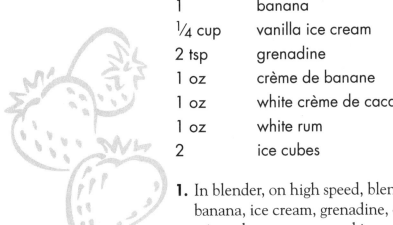

10	frozen strawberries	10
1	banana	1
¼ cup	vanilla ice cream	50 mL
2 tsp	grenadine	10 mL
1 oz	crème de banane	25 mL
1 oz	white crème de cacao	25 mL
1 oz	white rum	25 mL
2	ice cubes	2

1. In blender, on high speed, blend strawberries, banana, ice cream, grenadine, crème de banane, crème de cacao, rum and ice until smooth.

2. Pour into a milkshake glass or a tall stemmed punch glass.

Makes 1 serving

Madeira M'Dear Post-prandial Shake

6	fresh or frozen strawberries	6
¼ cup	vanilla ice cream	50 mL
2 oz	Madeira	25 mL
1	fresh strawberry (optional)	1

1. In blender, on high speed, blend strawberries, ice cream and Madeira until smooth.

2. Pour into an old-fashioned glass and garnish with strawberry, if desired.

Makes 1 serving

Strawberry Creamsicle Cocktail

6	frozen strawberries	6
¼ cup	vanilla ice cream	50 mL
1½ oz	Irish cream liqueur	40 mL
1 oz	vodka	25 mL
1	fresh strawberry (optional)	1

1. In blender, on high speed, blend frozen strawberries, ice cream, Irish cream liqueur and vodka until smooth.

2. Pour into an old-fashioned glass and garnish with fresh strawberry, if desired.

Makes 1 serving

Berry Mint Shake

12	fresh or frozen strawberries	12
1/4 cup	vanilla ice cream	50 mL
1 1/2 oz	white crème de menthe	40 mL
1 1/2 oz	framboise or raspberry vodka	40 mL
2	ice cubes	2

1. In blender, on high speed, blend strawberries, ice cream, crème de menthe, framboise and ice until slushy.
2. Pour into a highball glass.

Makes 1 serving

Peach-Almond Shake

TIP

To peel a fresh peach, submerge it in boiling water for 10 to 15 seconds to loosen the skin. Or use drained canned peaches or frozen sliced peaches.

1/2 cup	cubed peeled peaches (see tip, at left)	125 mL
1/3 cup	vanilla ice cream	75 mL
2 tsp	freshly squeezed lemon juice	10 mL
1 oz	brandy	25 mL
1 oz	peach schnapps	25 mL
1 oz	almond liqueur	25 mL
1	ice cube	1

1. In blender, on high speed, blend peaches, ice cream, lemon juice, brandy, peach schnapps, almond liqueur and ice until smooth.
2. Pour into an old-fashioned glass.

Makes 1 serving

Minty Grasshopper

Here's another emerald-hued drink for those looking for something to serve on St. Patrick's Day (see also Leaping Leprechauns, page 76) — or serve it anytime for dessert with a chocolate-covered mint.

½ cup	vanilla ice cream	125 mL
1 oz	green crème de menthe	25 mL
1 oz	Irish cream liqueur	25 mL

1. In blender, on high speed, blend vanilla ice cream, crème de menthe and Irish cream liqueur until smooth.

2. Pour into a piña colada or old-fashioned glass.

Makes 1 serving

Creamy White Grasshopper

You can further embellish this cocktail with a sprinkle of grated white chocolate.

¼ cup	vanilla ice cream	50 mL
¼ cup	light (5%) cream	50 mL
1 oz	white crème de menthe	25 mL
1 oz	white crème de cacao	25 mL
1	sprig fresh mint	1

1. In blender, on high speed, blend ice cream, cream, crème de menthe and crème de cacao until smooth.

2. Pour into a piña colada or old-fashioned glass and garnish with mint sprig.

Makes 1 serving

Serve this yummy shake instead of dessert.

Frosty Almond Shake

½ cup	vanilla ice cream	125 mL
1 oz	almond liqueur	25 mL
1 oz	coffee liqueur	25 mL

1. In blender, on high speed, blend ice cream, almond liqueur and coffee liqueur until smooth.

2. Pour into an old-fashioned glass or serve in an ice cream bowl with a straw.

Makes 1 serving

Serve this unusual sweet and creamy dessert cocktail with small crispy amaretti (Italian almond cookies).

Italian Cream

¼ cup	vanilla ice cream	50 mL
2 oz	Marsala wine	50 mL
1 oz	white crème de cacao	25 mL

1. In blender, on high speed, blend ice cream, Marsala and crème de cacao until smooth.

2. Pour into a martini glass.

Makes 1 serving

Hazelnut Cream

To top off this fancy dessert cocktail, serve it with a chocolate-covered hazelnut (such as Ferrero Rocher).

1/4 cup	vanilla ice cream	50 mL
1 oz	Irish cream liqueur	25 mL
1/2 oz	hazelnut liqueur	15 mL
1/2 oz	coffee liqueur	15 mL

1. In blender, on high speed, blend ice cream, Irish cream liqueur, hazelnut liqueur and coffee liqueur until smooth.

2. Pour into an old-fashioned glass.

Makes 1 serving

TIP

If you don't have almond milk on hand, replace it with 3 tbsp (45 mL) light (5%) cream and 2 tbsp (25 mL) slivered almonds.

Nutty Professor

1/2 cup	pralines and cream or vanilla ice cream	125 mL
1/4 cup	almond milk (see tip, at left)	50 mL
1 oz	almond liqueur	25 mL
1 oz	hazelnut liqueur	25 mL

1. In blender, on high speed, blend ice cream, almond milk, almond liqueur and hazelnut liqueur until smooth.

2. Pour into an old-fashioned glass.

Makes 1 serving

Golden Cadillac

¼ cup	vanilla ice cream	50 mL
1 oz	crème de cacao	25 mL
1 oz	Galliano	25 mL
1	maraschino cherry	1

1. In blender, on high speed, blend ice cream, crème de cacao and Galliano until smooth.

2. Pour into a martini glass and garnish with cherry.

Makes 1 serving

Velvet Hammer

¼ cup	vanilla ice cream	50 mL
1 oz	orange liqueur	25 mL
1 oz	white crème de cacao	25 mL
Dash	ground nutmeg	Dash

1. In blender, on high speed, blend ice cream, orange liqueur and crème de cacao until smooth.

2. Pour into a martini glass and sprinkle with nutmeg.

Makes 1 serving

Chocolate Cheesecake

¼ cup	chocolate ice cream	50 mL
3 tbsp	light (5%) cream	45 mL
1 tbsp	mascarpone or cream cheese	15 mL
1 ½ oz	crème de cacao	40 mL
1 oz	brandy	25 mL
½ oz	almond liqueur	15 mL

1. In blender, on high speed, blend ice cream, cream, mascarpone, crème de cacao, brandy and almond liqueur until smooth.

2. Pour into an old-fashioned glass.

Makes 1 serving

Truffle in a Glass

¼ cup	chocolate ice cream	50 mL
1 oz	hazelnut liqueur	25 mL
4	ice cubes	4
1 tsp	grated bittersweet chocolate (optional)	5 mL

1. In blender, on high speed, blend ice cream, hazelnut liqueur and ice until smooth.

2. Pour into an old-fashioned glass and sprinkle with chocolate, if desired.

Makes 1 serving

Mint Truffle Shake

¼ cup	chocolate ice cream	50 mL
1 oz	hazelnut liqueur	25 mL
½ oz	white crème de menthe	15 mL
4	ice cubes	4
1 tsp	grated bittersweet chocolate (optional)	5 mL

1. In blender, on high speed, blend ice cream, hazelnut liqueur, crème de menthe and ice until smooth.

2. Pour into an old-fashioned glass and sprinkle with chocolate, if desired.

Makes 1 serving

Frozen Mudslide

½ cup	vanilla ice cream	125 mL
½ cup	milk	125 mL
2 oz	Irish cream liqueur	50 mL
1 oz	coffee liqueur	25 mL
1 oz	vodka	25 mL
1	ice cube	1
1 tbsp	grated bittersweet chocolate	15 mL

1. In blender, on high speed, blend ice cream, milk, Irish cream liqueur, coffee liqueur, vodka and ice until smooth.

2. Pour into an old-fashioned glass and sprinkle with chocolate.

Makes 1 serving

Bullhorn

¼ cup	coffee ice cream	50 mL
1 tbsp	chocolate syrup	15 mL
1 oz	coffee liqueur	25 mL
1 oz	orange liqueur	25 mL
¼ cup	chilled cola	50 mL
1	slice orange	1

1. In blender, on high speed, blend ice cream, chocolate syrup, coffee liqueur and orange liqueur until smooth.

2. Pour into a piña colada glass and top with cola. Garnish with orange slice.

Makes 1 serving

Choco-Orange Cream

Sometimes even a cold coffee can give you a warm, fuzzy feeling.

½ cup	chocolate ice cream	125 mL
⅓ cup	chilled strong coffee or espresso	75 mL
1 oz	orange liqueur	25 mL
1 oz	crème de cacao	25 mL
2	ice cubes	2
1	slice orange	1

1. In blender, on high speed, blend ice cream, coffee, orange liqueur, crème de cacao and ice until smooth.

2. Pour into an old-fashioned glass and garnish with orange slice.

Makes 1 serving

Mochaccino

7	chocolate-covered espresso beans, divided	7
1/2 cup	chilled strong coffee or espresso	125 mL
1/2 cup	coffee or chocolate ice cream	125 mL
1/4 cup	chocolate milk or milk	50 mL
1/4 tsp	ground cinnamon, divided	1 mL
1 oz	coffee liqueur	25 mL
1 oz	Irish cream liqueur	25 mL
1	ice cube	1

1. In blender, on high speed, blend 4 of the espresso beans, coffee, ice cream, chocolate milk, a pinch of cinnamon, coffee liqueur, Irish cream liqueur and ice until smooth.

2. Pour into a highball glass, garnish with the remaining 3 coffee beans and sprinkle with the remaining cinnamon.

Makes 1 serving

Irish Cream Coffee

1/4 cup	cold brewed espresso coffee	50 mL
1/4 cup	chocolate ice cream	50 mL
3 oz	Irish cream liqueur	75 mL

1. In blender, on high speed, blend coffee, ice cream and Irish cream liqueur until smooth.

2. Pour into an old-fashioned glass or a coffee cup.

mocktails

WHETHER YOU ARE CATERING to teetotaling friends or to designated drivers, it's always a good idea to have some non-alcoholic drinks in your repertoire. These drinks also allow kids to join the party and feel like grown-ups. "Mocktails," while containing no alcohol, are similar to cocktails in appearance and flavor. The similarity is achieved through the use of chilled fruit nectars, frozen fruit juice concentrates, carbonated sodas and certain extracts. Dressed up with fresh fruit garnishes and umbrella straws, these drinks will have your sober guests partying in no time. The recipes provide enough for two drinks but can easily be doubled or tripled for a crowd.

MOCKTAIL RECIPES

Makes 2 servings

Morning Sunshine

For extra "sparkle," add a splash of grapefruit soda to each glass just before garnishing.

4	ice cubes	4
½ cup	orange juice	125 mL
½ cup	pink grapefruit juice	125 mL
2 tbsp	freshly squeezed lemon juice	25 mL
1 tsp	grenadine	5 mL
Pinch	ground cinnamon	Pinch
	Fresh mint leaves	

1. In blender, pulse ice until crushed. On high speed, blend in orange juice, grapefruit juice, lemon juice, grenadine and cinnamon until smooth.

2. Pour into 2 cocktail glasses and garnish with mint leaves.

Makes 2 servings

Apple Blossom

Variation

For a delicate citrus twist, replace the elderflower water with orange flower water.

4	ice cubes	4
1 cup	apple cider	250 mL
½ cup	elderflower water	125 mL
Pinch	freshly grated nutmeg	Pinch
	Cinnamon sticks	

1. In blender, pulse ice until crushed. On high speed, blend in apple cider, elderflower water and nutmeg until smooth.

2. Pour into 2 old-fashioned glasses and garnish with cinnamon sticks.

Little Miss Pink

This recipe contains a raw egg white. If the food safety of raw eggs is a concern for you, use the pasteurized egg white instead.

1	egg white (or 2 tbsp/25 mL pasteurized liquid egg white)	1
1 cup	cranberry cocktail	250 mL
¼ cup	raspberry cordial	50 mL
2 tsp	confectioner's (icing) sugar	10 mL

1. In blender, on high speed, blend egg white, cranberry cocktail, raspberry cordial and sugar until smooth and frothy.

2. Pour into 2 flutes.

Strawberry Squeeze

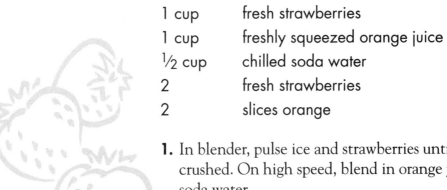

4	ice cubes	4
1 cup	fresh strawberries	250 mL
1 cup	freshly squeezed orange juice	250 mL
½ cup	chilled soda water	125 mL
2	fresh strawberries	2
2	slices orange	2

1. In blender, pulse ice and strawberries until ice is crushed. On high speed, blend in orange juice and soda water.

2. Pour into 2 cocktail or old-fashioned glasses and garnish each with a strawberry and an orange slice.

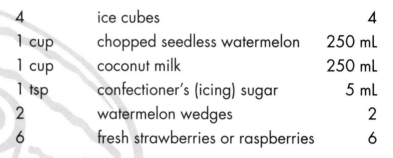

Makes 2 servings

Watermelon Whip

4	ice cubes	4
1 cup	chopped seedless watermelon	250 mL
1 cup	coconut milk	250 mL
1 tsp	confectioner's (icing) sugar	5 mL
2	watermelon wedges	2
6	fresh strawberries or raspberries	6

1. In blender, pulse ice until crushed. On high speed, blend in watermelon, coconut milk and sugar until smooth.

2. Pour into 2 highball glasses and garnish each with a watermelon wedge and 3 berries.

Makes 2 servings

Pineapple Delight

Variation

Substitute fresh or frozen strawberries for the pineapple.

1 cup	chopped pineapple	250 mL
¼ cup	sweetened condensed milk	50 mL
1 tsp	grenadine	5 mL
4	ice cubes	4
2	fresh strawberries	2
2	pineapple wedges	2

1. In blender, on high speed, blend pineapple, condensed milk, grenadine and ice until smooth.

2. Pour into 2 highball glasses and garnish each with a strawberry and a pineapple wedge.

Makes 2 servings

Piña Col-nada

Variation

For a different tropical treat, replace the pineapple and juice with chopped mango and ¼ cup (50 mL) mango nectar.

4	ice cubes	4
1 cup	coconut milk	250 mL
1 cup	canned crushed pineapple, with juice	250 mL
2	fresh strawberries	2

1. In blender, pulse ice until crushed. On high speed, blend in coconut milk, pineapple and pineapple juice until smooth.

2. Pour into 2 highball glasses and garnish each with a strawberry.

Makes 2 servings

Tropical Punch

4	ice cubes	4
½ cup	passion fruit juice (see tip, page 50)	125 mL
½ cup	mango nectar (see tip, page 50)	125 mL
½ cup	guava juice (see tip, page 51)	125 mL
1 tbsp	rum extract (optional)	25 mL
1 tbsp	freshly squeezed lime juice	25 mL
2	pineapple wedges	2

1. In blender, pulse ice until crushed. On high speed, blend in passion fruit juice, mango nectar, guava juice, rum extract (if using) and lime juice until blended.

2. Pour into 2 punch cups or cocktail glasses and garnish each with a pineapple wedge and an umbrella straw.

Makes 2 servings

Chocolate Monkey

This is the perfect beverage for your "little monkeys" on a hot afternoon by the pool.

4	ice cubes	4
1	banana, sliced	1
1 cup	chocolate milk	250 mL
½ cup	coconut milk	125 mL
2 tbsp	peanut butter	25 mL

1. In blender, pulse ice and banana until ice is crushed. On high speed, blend in chocolate milk, coconut milk and peanut butter until smooth.

2. Pour into 2 chilled highball glasses.

Makes 2 servings

Mock Caesar

4	ice cubes	4
1½ cups	tomato or tomato-clam juice	375 mL
1 tbsp	freshly squeezed lemon juice	15 mL
2 tsp	hot pepper sauce	10 mL
1 tsp	Worcestershire sauce	5 mL
Pinch	celery salt	Pinch
2	celery stalks	2

1. In blender, pulse ice until crushed. On high speed, blend in tomato juice, lemon juice, hot pepper sauce and Worcestershire sauce until smooth.

2. Pour into 2 highball glasses and sprinkle with celery salt. Garnish each glass with a celery stalk.

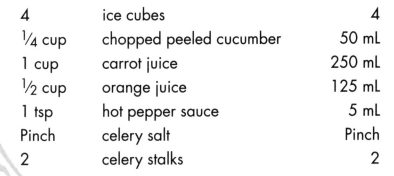

Makes 2 servings

Bugs Bunny

4	ice cubes	4
¼ cup	chopped peeled cucumber	50 mL
1 cup	carrot juice	250 mL
½ cup	orange juice	125 mL
1 tsp	hot pepper sauce	5 mL
Pinch	celery salt	Pinch
2	celery stalks	2

1. In blender, pulse ice and cucumber until ice is crushed. On high speed, blend in carrot juice, orange juice and hot pepper sauce.

2. Pour into 2 highball glasses and sprinkle with celery salt. Garnish each glass with a celery stalk.

Makes 2 servings

Summer's perfect flavor combination, blended together in this creamy concoction.

Strawberries and Cream

4	ice cubes	4
1 cup	sliced fresh strawberries	250 mL
½ cup	half-and-half (10%) cream or whole milk	125 mL
2 tsp	grenadine	10 mL
¼ tsp	grated lemon zest	1 mL
2	fresh strawberries	2
2	twists lemon rind	2

1. In blender, pulse ice and sliced strawberries until ice is crushed. On high speed, blend in cream, grenadine and lemon zest until smooth and creamy.

2. Pour into 2 highball glasses and garnish each with a strawberry and a lemon twist.

Makes 2 servings

Serenity

This mocktail gets its name from the calming properties that green tea, ginger and pear provide when blended together.

4	ice cubes	4
4	fresh mint leaves	4
1 cup	chilled brewed green tea	250 mL
½ cup	pear nectar (see tip, page 193)	125 mL
Pinch	ground ginger	Pinch

1. In blender, pulse ice until crushed. On high speed, blend in mint, green tea and pear nectar until smooth.

2. Pour into 2 old-fashioned glasses and sprinkle with ginger.

Makes 2 servings

Frappaccino

Every coffee shop has its own variation on this warm-weather favorite. Why not make your own for a fraction of the cost? Lower-fat milks will work but have a thinner consistency and a weaker flavor. Serve frappaccinos after dinner in demitasse cups with a cinnamon pizzelle.

4	ice cubes	4
1 cup	chilled brewed espresso coffee	250 mL
½ cup	half-and-half (10%) cream or whole milk	125 mL
2 tbsp	granulated sugar	25 mL
Pinch	ground cinnamon (optional)	Pinch

1. In blender, pulse ice until crushed. On high speed, blend in espresso, cream and sugar until smooth.

2. Pour into 2 chilled highball glasses and sprinkle with cinnamon, if desired.

Makes 2 servings

Mocha Mocha

4	ice cubes	4
1 cup	chilled brewed espresso coffee	250 mL
1/2 cup	chocolate milk	125 mL
1/4 cup	whipped cream	50 mL
	Grated bittersweet or semisweet chocolate	

1. In blender, pulse ice until crushed. On high speed, blend in espresso and chocolate milk until smooth.

2. Pour into 2 chilled highball glasses and garnish each with a dollop of whipped cream and a sprinkle of grated chocolate.

Makes 2 servings

Shirley Temple

The "original" virgin cocktail just wouldn't be complete without a maraschino cherry.

4	ice cubes	4
1 1/2 cups	chilled ginger ale	375 mL
1 tsp	grenadine	5 mL
2	slices orange	2
2	maraschino cherries	2
2	orange wedges	2

1. In blender, pulse ice until crushed. On high speed, blend in ginger ale and grenadine just to combine.

2. Pour into 2 old-fashioned glasses and float an orange slice on each. Garnish each glass with a skewered cherry and orange wedge.

Ginger Snap

If you're only mildly fond of ginger, strain this drink through a fine sieve to get rid of any bits of ginger. I like the zip they give.

4	ice cubes	4
1 tsp	minced fresh gingerroot	5 mL
1 ½ cups	chilled ginger beer or ginger ale	375 mL
1 tsp	grenadine	5 mL

1. In blender, pulse ice and ginger until ice is crushed. On high speed, blend in ginger beer and grenadine.

2. Pour into 2 chilled old-fashioned glasses.

Sangria for Beginners

2	ice cubes	2
1 cup	red grape juice	250 mL
½ cup	cranberry juice	125 mL
½ cup	chilled ginger ale	125 mL
4	slices orange	4

1. In blender, pulse ice until crushed. On high speed, blend in grape juice, cranberry juice and ginger ale until blended.

2. Pour into 2 highball glasses and float an orange slice on each.

Mock Champagne

The bubbles and sweetness combined with a hint of tartness will have you celebrating in sober style — perfect for underage graduates.

1 ½ cups	chilled ginger beer or ginger ale	375 mL
1 tbsp	frozen grapefruit juice concentrate	25 mL
1 tsp	grenadine	5 mL
¼ cup	chilled soda water	50 mL

1. In blender, on high speed, blend ginger beer, grapefruit juice concentrate and grenadine until smooth.

2. Pour into 2 flutes and top with soda.

Citrus Surprise

4	ice cubes	4
½ cup	chopped peeled cucumber	125 mL
1 cup	orange juice	250 mL
1 tsp	hot pepper sauce (or to taste)	5 mL
½ cup	chilled soda water	125 mL

1. In blender, pulse ice and cucumber until ice is crushed. On high speed, blend in orange juice and hot pepper sauce (add more if you like heat).

2. Pour into 2 highball glasses and top with soda.

Makes 2 servings

Pretender's Punch

4	ice cubes	4
½ cup	cranberry juice	125 mL
½ cup	orange juice	125 mL
½ cup	pineapple juice	125 mL
½ cup	chilled soda water	125 mL
2	lemon wedges	2

1. In blender, pulse ice until crushed. On high speed, blend in cranberry juice, orange juice and pineapple juice until smooth.

2. Pour into 2 highball glasses and top with soda. Garnish each glass with a lemon wedge.

Makes 2 servings

Peach Mock-ari

Variation

Substitute an equal amount of canned sliced pears and pear nectar for the peaches and peach nectar.

3	ice cubes	3
1 cup	frozen sliced peaches	250 mL
1 cup	peach nectar (see tip, page 190)	250 mL
½ cup	chilled lime-flavored sparkling water	125 mL
2	fresh peach wedges	2

1. In blender, pulse ice and frozen peaches until ice is crushed. On high speed, blend in peach nectar and sparkling water until smooth.

2. Pour into 2 chilled old-fashioned or martini glasses and garnish each with a peach wedge.

Makes 2 servings

Grape Fizz

2	ice cubes	2
1 cup	frozen green seedless grapes	250 mL
1 cup	white grape juice	250 mL
¼ cup	chilled soda water	50 mL

1. In blender, pulse ice and grapes until ice is crushed. On high speed, blend in grape juice until smooth.

2. Pour into 2 chilled old-fashioned glasses and top with soda.

Makes 2 servings

The sweetened condensed milk turns this classic beverage into a new family favorite.

Orange Julius

4	ice cubes	4
1 cup	frozen orange juice concentrate	250 mL
½ cup	milk	125 mL
¼ cup	sweetened condensed milk	50 mL
2	orange wedges (optional)	2

1. In blender, pulse ice until crushed. On high speed, blend in orange juice concentrate, milk and condensed milk until smooth.

2. Pour into 2 chilled old-fashioned glasses and garnish each with an orange wedge, if desired.

Makes 2 servings

Goosestopper

2	ice cubes	2
½ cup	orange juice concentrate	125 mL
1 cup	grapefruit juice	250 mL
Dash	angostura bitters	Dash
½ cup	chilled soda water	125 mL
2	slices orange	2

1. In blender, pulse ice until crushed. On high speed, blend in orange juice concentrate, grapefruit juice and bitters.

2. Pour into 2 highball glasses and top with soda. Garnish each glass with an orange slice.

Makes 2 servings

Fruit Punch

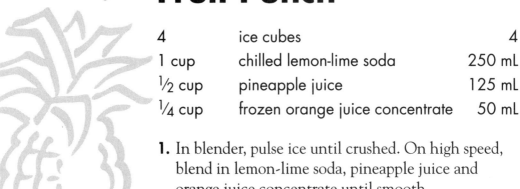

4	ice cubes	4
1 cup	chilled lemon-lime soda	250 mL
½ cup	pineapple juice	125 mL
¼ cup	frozen orange juice concentrate	50 mL

1. In blender, pulse ice until crushed. On high speed, blend in lemon-lime soda, pineapple juice and orange juice concentrate until smooth.

2. Pour into 2 chilled punch cups.

Lush Lemon

Makes 2 servings

This mocktail is everything a sexy drink should be. Serve it in chilled sake cups at your next prenatal get-together.

4	ice cubes	4
1 cup	coconut milk	250 mL
1/4 cup	frozen lemonade concentrate	50 mL
2	twists lemon rind	2

1. In blender, pulse ice until crushed. On high speed, blend in coconut milk and lemonade concentrate.

2. Pour into 2 highball glasses and garnish each with a lemon twist.

Minted Blue Cooler

Makes 2 servings

Frozen blueberries provide the spectacular color of this drink. Fresh berries taste fine, but the color is much less vibrant.

8	fresh mint leaves	8
1 1/2 cups	chilled soda water	375 mL
1/2 cup	frozen blueberries	125 mL
1/4 cup	frozen lemonade concentrate	50 mL
1 tsp	confectioner's (icing) sugar	5 mL
2	twists lemon rind	2

1. In blender, on high speed, blend mint, soda water, blueberries, lemonade concentrate and sugar until smooth.

2. Pour into 2 chilled old-fashioned glasses and garnish each with a lemon twist.

Makes 2 servings

Lime Rickey

The bitters help to round out this beverage, for the illusion of an alcoholic cocktail.

4	ice cubes	4
½ cup	frozen limeade concentrate	125 mL
Dash	angostura bitters	Dash
1 cup	soda water	250 mL
2	twists lime rind	2

1. In blender, pulse ice until crushed. On high speed, blend in limeade concentrate and bitters until smooth.

2. Pour into 2 highball glasses and top with soda. Garnish each glass with a lime twist.

Makes 2 servings

Peach Bliss

1 cup	frozen sliced peaches	250 mL
1 cup	chilled soda water	250 mL
¼ cup	frozen limeade concentrate	50 mL
2 tsp	confectioner's (icing) sugar	10 mL

1. In blender, on high speed, blend peaches, soda water, limeade concentrate and sugar until smooth.

2. Pour into 2 chilled old-fashioned glasses.

Makes 2 servings

Island Breeze

Ginger beer provides enough punch to hold its own with the cranberry and lime flavors. Milder ginger ale is good, but you might want to add a bit of grated ginger for an extra kick.

4	ice cubes	4
1 cup	cranberry juice	250 mL
1/2 cup	chilled ginger beer or ginger ale	125 mL
1/4 cup	frozen limeade concentrate	50 mL

1. In blender, pulse ice until crushed. On high speed, blend in cranberry juice, ginger beer and limeade concentrate.

2. Pour into 2 chilled highball glasses.

Makes 2 servings

Mock Mojito

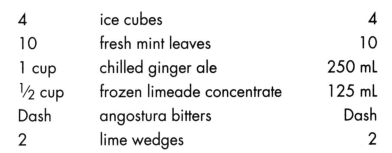

4	ice cubes	4
10	fresh mint leaves	10
1 cup	chilled ginger ale	250 mL
1/2 cup	frozen limeade concentrate	125 mL
Dash	angostura bitters	Dash
2	lime wedges	2

1. In blender, pulse ice until crushed. On high speed, blend in mint, ginger ale, limeade concentrate and bitters until smooth.

2. Pour into 2 old-fashioned glasses and garnish each with a lime wedge.

Makes 2 servings

Casual Cosmo

4	ice cubes	4
½ cup	white grape juice	125 mL
2 tbsp	frozen cranberry cocktail concentrate	25 mL
Dash	angostura bitters	Dash
¼ cup	chilled soda water	50 mL
6	frozen cranberries	6

1. In blender, pulse ice until crushed. On high speed, blend in grape juice, cranberry cocktail concentrate and bitters until smooth.

2. Pour into 2 martini glasses and top with soda. Garnish each glass with 3 frozen cranberries.

Makes 2 servings

Raspberry Burst

For variety, try different sorbets. Rainbow sorbet not only offers great flavor, but when a little scoop is added to each glass, it provides a visual treat as well.

1½ cups	white grape juice	375 mL
1 cup	raspberry sorbet	250 mL
10	fresh mint leaves, divided	10

1. In blender, on high speed, blend grape juice, sorbet and 8 of the mint leaves until smooth.

2. Pour into 2 chilled old-fashioned or martini glasses and garnish each with a mint leaf.

Makes 2 servings

Key Lime Kiss

1 cup	lime sorbet	250 mL
½ cup	vanilla ice cream	125 mL
1 tbsp	freshly squeezed key lime juice	15 mL
1 cup	chilled ginger ale	250 mL
2	key lime wedges	2

1. In blender, on high speed, blend sorbet, ice cream, key lime juice and ginger ale until smooth and frothy.

2. Pour into 2 chilled highball glasses and garnish each with a lime wedge.

Makes 2 servings

Vanilla Bean

Imagine a cola float all grown up... yum.

4	ice cubes	4
1 cup	vanilla ice cream	250 mL
1 cup	chilled cola	250 mL
2 tsp	vanilla	10 mL

1. In blender, pulse ice until crushed. On high speed, blend in ice cream, cola and vanilla until smooth.

2. Pour into 2 chilled old-fashioned glasses and serve with straws.

S'Nog

Makes 2 servings

This recipe contains raw egg yolks. If the food safety of raw eggs is a concern for you, use the pasteurized liquid whole egg instead.

2	egg yolks (or ¼ cup/50 mL pasteurized liquid whole egg)	2
1 cup	vanilla ice cream	250 mL
½ cup	milk	125 mL
¼ cup	frozen orange juice concentrate	50 mL
1 tbsp	rum extract (optional)	25 mL
Pinch	ground cinnamon	Pinch
Pinch	freshly grated nutmeg	Pinch

1. In blender, on high speed, blend egg yolks, ice cream, milk, orange juice concentrate and rum extract (if using) until smooth.

2. Pour into 2 eggnog cups or punch cups and sprinkle with cinnamon and nutmeg.

Baby Blue Lagoon

Makes 2 servings

This mocktail is ideal for your next beach/pool party — all the color with no hangover.

4	ice cubes	4
1 cup	vanilla ice cream	250 mL
1 cup	blueberry-flavored fruit drink	250 mL
½ cup	chilled soda water	125 mL
2	pineapple wedges	2

1. In blender, pulse ice until crushed. On high speed, blend in ice cream, fruit drink and soda water.

2. Pour into 2 highball glasses and garnish each with a pineapple-skewered umbrella.

Makes 2 servings

Mud Puddle

4	ice cubes	4
1 tbsp	instant coffee granules	15 mL
1 cup	vanilla ice cream	250 mL
1 cup	milk	250 mL
2 tbsp	grated bittersweet chocolate	25 mL

1. In blender, pulse ice and coffee until ice is crushed. On high speed, blend in ice cream and milk until smooth.

2. Pour into 2 chilled highball glasses and sprinkle with grated chocolate.

Makes 2 servings

After Eight

Serve this mocktail in small chocolate cups as an after-dinner treat.

1 ½ cups	chocolate milk	375 mL
1 cup	chocolate ice cream	250 mL
1 tbsp	mint-flavored syrup	15 mL
2	sprigs fresh mint	2

1. In blender, on high speed, blend chocolate milk, ice cream and mint syrup until smooth.

2. Pour into 2 highball glasses and garnish each with a mint sprig.

index

Library and Archives Canada Cataloguing in Publication

Chase, Andrew
    400 blender cocktails : sensational alcoholic and non-alcoholic cocktail recipes /
Andrew Chase, Alison Kent, Nicole Young.

Includes index.
ISBN-13: 978-0-7788-0142-9
ISBN-10: 0-7788-0142-X

1. Cocktails. 2. Blenders (Cookery). I. Kent, Alison II. Young, Nicole
III. Title. IV. Title: Four hundred blender cocktails.

TX951.C48 2006   641.8'74   C2006-902633-5